ZAPATA

OF MEXICO

**BLACK
ROSE
BOOKS**

Montréal/New York/London

Black Rose Books No. AA249
Hardcover ISBN: 1-55164-073-2 (bound)
Paperback ISBN: 1-55164-072-4 (pbk.)
Library of Congress Catalog Card Number: 96-79523

Canadian Cataloguing in Publication Data

Newell, Peter E.
Zapata of Mexico

Includes bibliographical references and index.
ISBN 1-55164-073-2 (bound).–
ISBN 1-55164-072-4 (pbk.)

1. Zapata, Emiliano, 1879-1919. 2. Mexico–
history–Rvolution, 1910-1920. 3. Revolutionaries–
Mexico–biography. I. Title.

F1234.N48 1997   972.08'16'092 c900780-9

BLACK
ROSE
BOOKS

C.P. 1258	250 Sonwil Drive	99 Wallis Road
Succ. Place du Parc	Buffalo, New York	London, E9 5LN
Montréal,Québec	14225 USA	England
H2W 2R3 Canada		

To order books in North America: (phone) 1-800-565-9523 (fax) 1-800-221-9985
In Europe: (phone) 081-986-4854 (fax) 081-533-5821

Our Web Site address: http://www.web.net/blackrosebooks

A publication of the Institute of Policy Alternatives of Montréal (IPAM)
Printed in Canada

CONTENTS

Eufemio Zapata, left, and his brother, Emiliano, right, in
the Hall of Ambassadors, National Palace, Mexico City.

Acknowledgements

I wish to thank Robert Kern of the University of New Mexico, Albuquerque, and of the University of Mexico City, who first discussed with me the idea of writing a book on Emiliano Zapata and the evolution of the *ejidal* lands, and for supplying me with a comprehensive list of works on the subject; and Mary Canipa of Freedom Press for obtaining various books, and for loaning me other works from the Tom Keel Library.

I also wish to thank Michael Malet, Nicolas Walter and Vero Richards, who read the first draft, and made a number of suggestions and comments, some of which I hope, I have accepted. Thanks also to Nita Luna of the Chicano Communications Center, Albuquerque, for answering a number of my questions.

P.E.N.

In Memory of My Mother,
Agnes W. Newell (1897 — 1976),
An Indomitable Spirit And
Fighter To The End.

Dear earth of ours! We pray thee:
Give back the corn we pay thee!
O holy corn, by moon, by morn,
Grow strong, grow tall, grow gaily
O Tierra Chica Mia!

HANGED MEN

CHAPTER I

EMILIANO

MORELOS, named after Jose Maria Morelos y Pavon, is one of the smallest states of Mexico. It is only about two hundred kilometres wide from border to border in any direction. But it is of great strategic importance. Its northernmost border lies less than one hundred kilometres south of Mexico City. It is known as the *patria chica* – the Little Fatherland.

In the north of the state there are the mighty mountain peaks of the Sierra Ajusco, rising more than 3,400 metres, and dividing it from the Valley of Mexico. Interspersed between the mountains are racing streams and small valleys. To the west are the peaks of the Sierra Judipero. Moving south, the mountains give way to undulating hills with rich vegetation – chimoyas, mameyes, zalotes and bananas – a dulcet land, moist, warm, semi-tropical, not forty kilometres from the low southern hotlands of steaming jungle, malaria and deadly heat. Further south still, the jungle gives way to the beautiful Valley of Morelos, with its hot sun, often followed by torrential rains which, in turn, make the earth green and fresh.

In the Valley of Morelos, herds of mules and horses can be seen grazing. But more importantly, sugar cane grows in abundance.

The men and women of Morelos are an ancient people. Who they are is one of Mexico's many mysteries. They have been called Tlahuicas, though that was not their original name. Presumably they are an offshoot of the Toltec-Chichimec amalgam of tribes which occupied the Valley of Morelos between the seventh and twelth centuries. But whatever their origin, the Morelenses are neither peasants in the European sense nor Indians in the North American sense, but apparently the remnants of an ancient civilisat - ion. They lived in their warm, well-watered valleys centuries before the arrival of the power-hungry Aztecs into Central Mexico.

For the most part, and despite centuries of oppression (with the rise of the Aztec Confederacy in the fifteenth century, the 'Tlahuicas' became a subject people, ceding much of their ancestral lands, which they held in common, to the new Aztec overlords), they still bear the marks of fine breeding: singularly large, dark, slightly odalisk eyes, perfect white teeth — the dogtooth bred out to flat incisor — finely articulated small hands and feet, slender, wiry physiques, with soft musical voices.

The Morelenses are instinctively courteous. Yet for the most part they are illiterate *peones* — People of the Earth. Ordinarily stoical and gentle, they are suspicious and distrustful of outsiders; and once roused they become fierce fighters. Indeed, some observers have called them child-like, as they appear to attach little importance to human life, either of their own or their enemies. Outside of their Valley of Morelos they have few friends and many enemies. They have a strong communal spirit, yoked to a mystical passion for the land and village. Traditionally, the Morelenses had no clear concept of private ownership: the land belonged — or should have belonged — to everyone who wanted it. They have often been despised by their neighbours, despite their ancient civilisation.

Yet as time went by, they too have to some extent mixed with their conquerers and oppressors.

SINCE the sixteenth century, sugar plantations dominated the life of Morelos. For in Morelos, the great *hacendados* mainly produced sugar cane but, unlike elsewhere in Mexico, they were interested in production for the market, for a profit, and not for immediate consumption. By 1870, machines were being introduced which extracted a much higher proportion of sugar from the stalk. Furthermore, the planters also began to build railroads — the Central Mexican and the Interocean — across the state and northwards, through the great Cima Divide, right into the heart of Mexico City itself.

Before 1870, there was oppression in Morelos as elsewhere in Mexico, but in the main the various classes and communities co-existed fairly amicably. Traditional *pueblos,* small farm settlements and *ejidos,* independent *ranchos, haciendas* and towns were scattered throughout the state. All did not flourish, but they mainly survived. Occasionally, a plantation owner would take over a village field if the *peones* were particularly unguarded. And some villagers were forced to migrate. But between 1870 and 1880 change became more rapid.

*

After 1880, many plantations and *haciendas* developed into 'company' towns, employing anything from 250 to 3,000 workers. Some planters organised their own stores, power-houses, schools and even police on the American method; they employed not only *peones* who worked in the cane-fields, but bricklayers, blacksmiths, carpenters, electricians and mechanics. They recruited their managers and overseers, and some of their skilled workers, from Mexico City, Cuba and Spain.

Throughout the 1880's, the Mexican government sold to the *hacendados* much of the common land left in the state, and also granted them favourable rulings on requests for titles to other requisitions. New Federal legislation jeopardised the previously held titles and water rights of many villages. Local courts approved dubiously-claimed appropriations.

By 1890, several important towns which were surrounded by plantations ceased to grow and, in a number of instances, actually declined. In the countryside outside the towns, especially in Yautepec, small old-fashioned *haciendas* failed and then were merged into larger, modern enterprises of a purely capitalist nature. Even whole villages began to disappear. Isolated ones in the north of the state — particularly in the mountains — remained safe, but those near the railway lines, timber forests or well-watered areas were very vulnerable.

In the year that General Porfirio Diaz took power, there were one hundred-and-eighteen *pueblos* recorded in Morelos; yet by 1887, despite an overall increase in population, there were scarcely one hundred-and-five. In Tequesquittengo, for example, the villagers had in some way or another offended the owner of the nearby San Jose Vista Hermosa plantation. He retaliated by running his irrigation water into the village lake, and flooding the whole *pueblo*. Only the spire of the church remained above water. Throughout the 1890's, and after the turn of the century, *pueblos* continued to die. And by 1909, less than one hundred were registered in Morelos. Hidden in the fields of high, green sugar-cane were the ruins of Acatlipa, Ahuehuepan, Cuauchichinola and many other villages. The villlagers were often involved in attempts to save them. The small town of Villa de Ayala declined from over 2,100 souls in 1899 to less than 1,700 by 1909; and Zapata's own village of Anenecuilco lost more than fifty people over the same period.

Little by little the *peones* lost their *ejidos,* pastures, water supplies and common lands. Ineluctably, they were driven into debt peonage, and into the cane fields of the great *hacendados* and planters.

11

Dispossessed and destitute, many villagers began sharecropping the scrubbiest of the plantation fields; then, when their debts mounted, they too were forced to hire themselves out to the *hacendados* as field hands, sometimes still living in their *pueblos*, but working in contracted gangs under a foreman. By Mexican standards of the time, a few often earned high wages — sixty-five *centavos* a day in the dry winter season, and as much as one *peso* during the Spring harvest. But they also found prices very high, particularly in the company stores which, in most cases, were the only stores in the district. Moreover, Morelos produced only sugar, rice and some rum in reasonable amounts; corn, beans and cotton materials, as well as some other staples, had to be imported into the state from Mexico City, Puebla and elsewhere. The workers, therefore, fell deeper and deeper into debt. Finally, many left the villages for good and, like the ex-*rancheros,* moved with their families on to the plantations as *gente de casa* — permanent, resident wage labourers. There on the *real* , if they did not 'step out of line', they could at least count on the bare necessities of life. Thus, besides acquiring more land, the planters of Morelos also acquired a dependent and, they hoped, docile labour force. To the planters it was a considerable advantage to have the workers settled on their *haciendas* rather than in the villages.

After the turn of the century, economic pressures on the planters and *hacendados* increased considerably. There was more intense competition within Mexico for the protected sugar market; and, furthermore, the production of sugar exceeded the domestic demand. In 1902, exporting began, but the costs of production in Morelos were still higher than elsewhere; and the international market lurched from one crisis to another. Also alarming was the threat of a growing native beet-sugar production, which the planters assumed would eventually destroy them. Throughout the period, moreover, the constant cultivation of cane was exhausting the soil. So the boom which began round about 1878, began to level off around 1908. All this increased pressure drove the planters to greater investments, either to diversify the grades of refined sugar or to produce more rum. They therefore, bought more machinery; and, to keep this machinery working, they had to grow yet more and more cane. And as they took more of the scrubbier land from the *peones*, so they required more water for irrigation.

By 1908, the seventeen owners of the thirty-six major *haciendas* in the state owned over twenty-five per cent of all the cultivatable land; and their twenty-four mills accounted for well over a third of Mexico's sugar production. After Hawaii and Puerto Rico, Morelos was the most productive sugar cane region in the world. Between 1905 and 1908, the Morelos planters increased production by over fifty per cent. And they put more and more pressure on the remaining 'free' *peones* and *rancheros*. Nevertheless, the *peones* and *rancheros* began to resist.

In 1903, Pablo Escandon directed the manager of his family's Atlihuayan *hacienda* to put up a fence which took about 1,500 hectares of Yautepec's communal pasture lands. The *peones'* cattle, used to grazing on it, broke through the fence in places, trampled it down and wandered back into the area taken by Escandon. The *hacienda* guards impounded the cattle and returned them to the villagers only on payment of a stiff fine. A number of *peones* were jailed for letting their beasts trespass. But the villagers were determined not to quit their common lands. After months of protesting without redress, they chose a local *ranchero,* Jovito Serrano, to represent them before the local authorities. Serrano first took the complaint to the Yautepec Court – which ruled against him. He then went to the Yautepec *jefe politico.* And when the *jefe* refused to review the Court's decision, Serrano appealed to the Cuernavaca District Court, which also upheld the original decision and, furthermore, imposed a seventy-*pesos* fine on the plaintiffs. Serrano then appealed to the country's Supreme Federal Court. But it was to no avail. As a last resort, the villagers decided to send a seventy-five strong delegation to President Diaz himself. They chartered a special train to Mexico City. Serrano led the delegation. Don Porfirio, as President Diaz liked to be called, welcomed them into his library at Chapultepec Castle. He told them that they were his children, listened to their story, said how sympathetic he was, gave them the name and address of another lawyer, a good friend of his, and told them that they must be patient – and the law would take its course. It did. The *peones* never did get their land back.

But among the delegation who went to see the President was a young man named Emiliano Zapata . . .

Elsewhere, in Coatlan de Rio, Jantetelco, Santa Maria, Tepalcingo and many other *pueblos,* the *peones* defied their local *hacendados* and planters in an attempt to defend and retain their *ejidos* and common lands. But, as in Yautepec, it was to no avail. They were either beaten up by the *hacienda* guards, conscripted into the Federal

13

Army or merely murdered by the dreaded *rurales*. Indeed, while Jovito Serrano was in Mexico City, he was arrested and jailed, and all his Yautepecan land titles, which proved the *peones'* rights to the land, were seized. The last that was heard of him was that he had been shipped to a concentration camp in Quintana Roo, together with thirty-five other *peones* and *rancheros* from Morelos.

But, in fact, 1909 was the turning point. Gone were the times when the *peones* would merely plead with the *hacendados,* or send representatives to the *jefe politicos,* or the District Court or even to Diaz. Resentment, more often than not, was turning to hatred. The only course open to the ordinary people was some kind of direct action.

EMILIANO ZAPATA, the ninth of ten children, was born on August 8, 1879, in the ancient village commune of San Miguel Anencuilco, near the town of Villa de Ayala and not very far from the *hacienda* of Chinameca, in the Valley of Morelos. He was almost pure 'Tlahuican', though the Zapata family had some Spanish 'blood'. The name Zapata means a leather hinge. It was an important name in San Miguel Anencuilco. One of Emiliano's Spanish ancestors rode with Cortes to the conquest of Tenochtitlan, and another is said to have served under Pizarro when he destroyed the Inca Empire of Peru. At the time of Emiliano Zapata's birth, some of the older members of the family still remembered, and had been involved in, the War of Independence against the French in the late 1860's.

Of the ten children born to Emiliano's mother, Cleofas, only four lived to adulthood. There were the two sisters, Jesucita and Luz, and the two brothers, Eufemio and Emiliano. Eufemio was five years older than Emiliano.

Although closely identified with Anencuilco and, in many ways, sharing with its folk the common tragedy of the lost lands, the Zapata family were not themselves *peones*, but *rancheros.* From father to son, for generations, they had owned and worked a modest *rancho* bordering both sides of the Rio Ayala. Almost all of the good tilth and pasture on the east bank had gone to swell the sugar-cane land of the neighbouring *hacienda*, but a tree-bowered portion on the western bank of the neighbouring *Sierra* remained a family possession.

For pasture, there still remained the green barrancas of the Sierra Ayala. And on their wild slopes young Emiliano gained his first experience with rope and rein, tending his father's spindly herd of

14

steers and kine. Little corn or beans could be raised, but there was always a brisk sale in near-by Cuautla for the locally famous Zapata cheese and butter. Horsemanship was a family tradition; and the breaking and training of colts provided a trickle of income. In the neighbouring strips of semi-jungle the family chickens, turkeys, goats and pigs picked up their own feed.

And, thus, the Zapata family's standard of living may have been depressed, but unlike many of the villagers, it was not depressed to the verge of want. There was even enough for an occasional luxury. If tortillas — thin, unleavened pancakes of ground corn and lime water — and beans were their staple diet, the Zapatas, unlike most of their neighbours, knew the taste of their own cheese, butter, eggs, milk and, sometimes, meat. And if in working hours, Gabriel Zapata, the father, and the boys went clad in coarse cotton shirts and pantaloons tied at the ankle; and the mother and girls in cotton undershift, blouse and skirt, they somehow managed to ride clad well enough to market, fair or *fiesta*. Then, the girls donned bright skirts and home-embroidered blouses, and the menfolk tight-fitting kersey-mere breeches adorned with silver buttons down the seam, lawn shirts and flowing ties, chamois jackets braided with gold thread, seamless one-piece *charro* boots and cartwheel, felt, sombreros, likewise braided. Even saddles and riding gear were mounted with the cheap silver mined in the state. And there usually was a carefully saved *peso* or two in Gabriel's pocket for a glass of *pulque* or *mezcal* with a friend, or to buy *dulces* for the girls.

To the Morelense *rancheros,* such small luxuries and adornments were stark necessities. Cheerfully they would slave, and even stint food, to secure them.

The Zapata family lived in a solid but small adobe-and-stone hut. It was little more than five metres by four metres, with a kitchen running the length of one side some two metres wide. The floor was earth, the walls adobe mud and the roof grass thatch; a simple square hole, without glass or shutter, provided a window. For many years the family lived, ate and slept in one room. Later, as the girls began to grow up, bedrooms of wattle and thatch were thrown on to the main part of the hut.

Life was primitive; a daily struggle with the simplest needs, and against longest odds. For Cleofas and the girls, there was the endless grinding of corn in the stone *metate* to supply the daily stack of tortillas, the endless laundering of white cotton shirts, skirts and pantaloons in the soft snow water of the Rio Ayala — to say nothing of the constant washing, combing and brushing of their fine, black manes of waist-long hair; the endless tending of clay pots on the smouldering coke of *brasero;* the milking, and churning of butter and cheese; and the endless fight, aided only by palm-leaf brooms, against dust and dirt around the house.

For Gabriel and the boys there was the tending of stock and the burning of lime in the hills; in season, the planting, hoeing and watering of scattered garden patches among the rocks, and the cutting and haul - ing of wild hay. For them, only on a Sunday or a *fiesta* was there the chance to ride abroad in their best clothes, and display their horsemanship. San Miguel Anencuilco was a quiet little place in those days.

The Zapata brothers, unlike most of the village children, had a little schooling. Emiliano spent about two years at Villa de Ayala's rather forlorn school. But he could only just read and write by the time he left, at about twelve years of age. He was, however, a good listener and learner throughout his life. And he soon learnt to hate the *hacendados.* Indeed, even his teacher at the Ayala school appears to have been a somewhat radical critic of the *hacienda* system. At the age of nine, Emiliano witnessed the last eviction of Anenecuilco's *peones* from their little huts and plots of land, and the enclosure of a village orchard; and he saw his father break down and cry. 'When I am a man, *mi padre*, I will put an end to this', he said. He told his father that, one day, he would get all the land back.

When Emiliano Zapata was eighteen, his father died. There was no priest or religious service at the funeral; nor was Don Gabriel buried in 'holy' ground. Zapata's father was a liberal and a freethinker. Eleven months later his mother, Dona Cleofas, also died. Eufemio and Emiliano jointly inherited the *rancho* and hut.

Jesucita, the eldest daughter, had already left home, and had married a young muleteer. And Eufemio, big and brawny, a heavy drinker and a heartless womanizer, went first to Veracruz peddling and hawking, and then to Orizba as a fruit merchant. Later, he married. Luz, Emiliano's younger sister, who had been keeping house since the death of the mother, also married and left the *rancho*. But Emiliano stayed at home, worked the land alone, sharecropped an extra hectare or two belonging to a local *hacendado* and, in slack times, ran a string of mules through the settlements of Cuautla. He bought and sold mules and, occasionally, horses in a small way. He was a natural horseman. He was also a crack shot. And he knew every trail, cave, ledge and hidden valley for hundreds of kilometres around.

16

He worked like his mules. He had boundless energy, and was very strong. He was as tough as nails.

Emiliano Zapata was a smallish, slender man with an opaque, rather expressionless yet sensuous and often sad face. He had large black, obsidian eyes and short untidy hair. He had big, slightly drooping, mandarin-type moustaches. He could be both cruel and ruthless to an enemy; though he was no sadist. He had great strength of character, was intelligent, frank, accesible, quick to understand people's problems and difficult to deceive. He became a good organiser, but was always a bad orator. Indeed, he was a fairly quiet man, who drunk less than most Mexicans, and became even quieter when he did drink. Yet he was, like many young *rancheros*, something of a dandy. On saints' days and holidays, Emiliano Zapata would ride to market or *fiesta* immaculately groomed. He would dress up, *charro*-style, all in black, or in a short leather jacket embroidered with gold thread, with tight fitting trousers complete with silver trimming down the seams, and an enormous silver-laden sombrero. And he would ride a fine black or white, silver-saddled, horse. He was the young *magnifico*. Zapata was the *charro* of *charros*!

It was at fair and *fiesta* that Zapata won his first fame.

Cuautla was a quiet, dull, town all the week, but Sunday was market day; and on Sunday the *plaza* was alive with thousands of people and hundreds of stalls, selling plums from Tlayacopan, chirmoyas from Tolopan, limes from Jonactepec, oranges from Yautepec, bananas from Oaxtepec, pottery from Cuernavaca and much more besides. There was an orchestra; and there was, above all, a rodeo. Here, early in his teens, Emiliano Zapata rode king; be it backing a bucking bull or *'la coleada en pelo'* — the trick of seizing a racing steer by the tail and throwing him on his back from a naked horse — or *'el paseo de la muerte'* — the perilous stunt of leaping at a mad gallop from a barebacked mount to the withers of a wild bronco, and riding him out — none could compete with him. He was the favourite of the *fiesta* crowds.

Naturally, the girls pursued him. Not only was he the *magnifico*; he was also the *romantico*. Emiliano Zapata enjoyed the company of beautiful women, and they enjoyed his company. Incapable of mere sensuality, he invariably became emotionally involved. Each affair became a small tragedy. Each left its scar. Unlike most *romanticos* of Mexico, Zapata had a conscience. And when a baby came along — as sometimes one did — he would dutifully provide

17

Genovivo de la O.

Eufemio Zapata

for it. He was a considerate and, indeed, a gentle lover.

But young Emiliano Zapata soon came into conflict with authority, sometimes defending fellow villagers against the *hacendados* or the *rurales*. Several times he had to leave the village in a hurry, and go into hiding for a while. He was only seventeen the first time his activities forced him on the run. Conflict with authority also hardened him.

CHAPTER II

DIAZ THE DICTATOR

In 1869, the Third Military District of the State of Mexico became the 'independent' State of Morelos. And in 1896, Manuel Alarcon, a Diaz puppet and local strong man, had himself 'elected' Governor. But in December, 1908, Alarcon, having been 'elected' for the fourth consecutive time, died.

Picking another Governor should not have been difficult. Four likely candidates were mentioned — and then turned down. Another name, Pablo Escandon, was mentioned. He was a 'model' *hacendado*, and a well-known sportsman who had been educated at Stonyhurst College in England, and who spent most of his time abroad. He was considered a ridiculous choice. But he was the planters' choice and, after some misgivings, he became Diaz's choice as well. The *Porfirista* political machine, therefore, slipped into gear. However, for the first time a local opposition began to form. The traders, artisans and 'white collar' workers of the Morelos towns — and, to a lesser degree, the people of the countryside — united against Escandon. They decided to chose a candidate of their own, General Francisco Leyva, a local hero of the War of Independence, and the state's first Governor. But Leyva refused to stand because he was, he said, an old man. He suggested his son, Patricio, an employee of the Federal Ministry of Works in Mexico City. He accepted; and various radicals and liberals from the capital and elsewhere pledged Patricio their support.

On January 22, 1909, the first large demonstration ever to be held in Morelos — over 1,500 people — was held in Cuautla. It was to celebrate the formation of the *Leyvista* Liberal Club. It was a great success. Crowds jammed the town's streets, cheering General Leyva and his son. And all over the eastern and central part of Morelos, the people took heart and followed Cuautla's lead.

In Villa de Ayala, just on thirty kilometres from Cuautla, a *Leyvista* club called the Melchor Ocampo, named after the famous nineteenth-century radical, was formed. Among its first members was Emiliano Zapata.

Political meetings began to attract large crowds all over the state. There was some rioting in Cuautla. The town's *Leyvista* club attempted to stage a rally on Sunday, January 22. The *jefe politico*, however, refused permission, but allowed a meeting the following Sunday afternoon. Members of *Leyvista* clubs from all over the area, including Villa de Ayala, went to Cuautla. Zapata, dressed 'to kill' in his finest *charro* outfit, rode into town on his famous black gelding, Pavon. Despite provocations by the local *jefe*, who posted *rurales* all round the square where the meeting was held, it was both peaceful and successful. But the next day, Escandon's supporters from Mexico City arrived in town by special train. The crowd was not particularly sympathetic, as it was a workday, and many of the workers had been forced to attend the meeting by their employers. A few rocks and stones were thrown at the platform. Federal troops then moved into the *plaza* and throughout the rest of the day many people, including a few local businessmen and traders, were arrested and taken off to jail. Sporadic arrests followed for days. Patricio Leyva, the opposition candidate, was fired from his job in the Ministry.

The 'election' which followed was, of course, a complete farce. The Federal Government drafted in a large contingent of *rurales*. The state's *jefe politicos* took control of the situation, and jailed many more oppositionists early on polling day. They also rigged the ballots. Federal troops stood on alert in every district of Morelos. And the result? Victory for Escandon. Of course! On March 15, Pablo Escandon went to Mexico City and was officially sworn in as Morelos' new Governor.

Late in the summer of 1909, however, a far more important election was held in Morelos. But no one realised that at the time. Moreover, it was not rigged; indeed, it was completely free. It was the election for the council, president and defence committee of the village commune of San Miguel Anencuilco. Such elections had taken place in the village − and many other villages of Central Mexico − for over seven hundred years.

During the evening dusk of a Sunday late in September, all the men of the village − who had previously been summoned quietly by word-of-mouth, so as not to alert the *hacienda* foreman, by the village elder, Jose Merino – assembled behind the church. Old Jose Merino quietly listed all the problems facing the villagers, including the sequestration of their common *ejido* lands, and told them that, in his view, they needed younger men to represent them. They agreed with him. A number of younger men were nominated, and duly elected to the village council. Nominations were then called for a president of the council and the defence committee. First, some-one nominated Modesto Gonzalez. Zapata nominated Bartolo Parral who, in turn, nominated Zapata. A vote was called for, and Emiliano Zapata was elected almost unanimously. Zapata, now thirty years and one month old, became the *caudillo* and chief representative of the village of San Miguel Anencuilco. That he had already had a number of brushes with authority was in his favour. Zapata, who was never called Don Emiliano, but always 'Miliano', was respected by everyone.

Throughout 1909, unrest continued to grow in Morelos. Guerrilla bands began to form. Most were poorly armed, and still quite small. One such group, led by the very independent village chief, Genovevo de la O, formed in the mountains north of Cuernavaca, had only twenty-five men and one .70 calibre musket. During the 'election', *rurales* had attempted to arrest de la O, but he escaped into the mountains. Nevertheless, they took his wife and two young daughters as hostages.

As more and more *insurrectos* appeared throughout the state, Governor Escandon found that neither the *rurales* nor the Federal Army could catch or crush them. And in their mountain hideouts they would, half-jokingly and half-seriously, shout: *'Viva la revolucion!'*, and then start singing the famous revolutionary song, *Adelita*.

> And if sounds forth the bugle to battle,
> And rides your guerrilla to war,
> And the blood runs bright in the mountains
> That despots may plague us no more . . . . .'

They had heard it a thousand times before, in the *plazas*, and at *fiestas*; but now it took on a new meaning.

More disturbing to the authorities, however, was that almost every *pueblo* in Morelos and the surrounding states was engaged in a dispute of some kind with its neighbouring *hacienda*. Of the hundred *pueblos* in Morelos in 1910, there was probably not one that had not been involved in an embittered legal dispute with its *hacienda*. Conflict was most

21

acute in the Cuautla area. The four farming communities in this municipality had been struggling for years against the encroachments of the Hospital and Cuahuixla *haciendas*. And the people there were probably more determined to defend themselves than anywhere else in the state. The village commune of San Miguel Anencuilco formed part of that municipality.

Following their election in September, 1909, Zapata and the new village council of Anencuilco began the old procedure of studying the village land titles. At first, they looked for a sympathetic lawyer, but could not find one. Zapata then sought advice in Mexico City from Paulino Martinez, an opponent of President Diaz; he also tried to contact one of the Flores Magon brothers, Jesus, but again without success.

Emiliano Zapata was now becoming more than a thorn in the side of the powers-that-be. He would have to be eliminated or, at least, removed from the Morelos scene. He was taken into custody, and was given the usual choice — a firing squad or being drafted into the Federal Army. On February 11, 1910, having decided that it would be better to remain alive, he was inducted into the Ninth Cavalry Regiment of the Mexican Army, stationed at the Morelos state capital of Cuernavaca. He became a *soldado*; and was immediately promoted to the rank of sergeant. The name of Emiliano Zapata was already widely known as that of a brilliant horseman.

But he did not remain long in the army. The wealthy *hacendado* and son-in-law of president Diaz, Ignacio de la Torre y Mier, wanted such a man as chief groom and general factotum in his Mexico City stables.

He wanted Zapata. And Don Ignacio always got what he wanted. By March 29, he had obtained Zapata's discharge from the Federal Army.

Emiliano Zapata went to Mexico City. And started working for Don Ignacio. He was surprised and shocked at what he saw. For the first time in his life he was brought face-to-face with grandeur, power, privilege and immense wealth. Mexico City was at its zenith. The streets were full of carriages, with coachmen and footmen, and brand new American automobiles. On Sunday afternoons, 'society' went to the bullfights — dedicated to the Virgin Mary! And night after night, week in and week out, there were society balls. In the words of Mrs. Leone B. Moats, the wife of a wealthy American businessman living in the city at the time, there were 'long rooms rimmed with mothers dressed in black, their hair, ears and necks bedecked with diamonds. Electric lights in crystal chandeliers. A crowded floor. Gusts of perfume. Large-bosomed women elegantly dressed from Paris. Elderly diplomats laden in decorations. And then the important part – many, many well-groomed young men who danced beautifully. Girls who giggled. Throbbing music. Gold furniture, invariably upholstered in pinkish plush. Mile upon mile of huge gold-framed mirrors, multiplying the spectacle.'

Invariably the balls and parties were large. Dinners ran to a hundred-and-fifty places, and gold plates were by no means unusual. Picnics were also conducted on the same elaborate and lavish scale, often served by four to six servants at a table. Then there was the Jockey Club . . . the Polo Club . . . the Automobile Club . . . and so on. Such was Mexico City.

Emiliano Zapata had never seen anything like it before. And, moreover, he did not like what he saw. Meanwhile, back in San Miguel Anencuilco the villagers were, once again, in dispute with the local *hacendado*. Zapata decided that it was time for him to escape from Mexico City, and return to his village. He was needed there. And he had had more than enough of the bright lights of the capital anyway. One night he quietly left . . . .

Throughout the spring of 1910, the *peones* of Anencuilco were in conflict with the Hospital *hacienda*. The villagers had compiled a new real-estate law, which allowed them to reclaim certain fields then in possession of the planter. He warned them that if they took over the fields he would drive them out. The villagers pleaded with him, and with various authorities, but delay followed delay. Just as they were getting desperate, Zapata returned from Mexico City. He immediately summoned the council and defence committee; and they decided that, as legal means had not proved successful, they would have to act for themselves. A group of about eighty men, some of whom were armed, including Zapata, went to the *hacienda*; the field guards retreated, and the villagers divided the fields into lots. The Anencuilcoans had won the first round. The news of their action soon spread around the state. For a few months the *peones* of San Miguel Anencuilco were left alone. But Zapata sent a delegation to President Diaz who, surprisingly, gave them a favourable ruling; and the local *jefe* passed it on to both Zapata and the *hacienda*

23

manager, who, though he did not like it, decided that he could do nothing – at least for the time being.

In mid-November, the *jefe politico*, Jose Vivanco, resigned under pressure from the *hacendados*, and his place was taken by one Eduardo Flores, who always took the side of the planters and big *hacendados*. But the *peones* were now on the move. Many of them, as well as the *campesinos* and *rancheros* from further south, supported the Anencuilco defence committee. In each disputed area, *hacienda* fences were torn down, and the people took over the land. The defence committee, which now included Villa de Ayala as well, could call upon about one hundred men who were prepared to act – and act quickly – on behalf of the *peones*.

By January, 1911, the *Zapatistas* (as they were soon to be called) were in effective control of a sizeable area of country around San Miguel Anencuilco and Villa de Ayala. It was, moreover, an area of strategic importance. The *Zapatistas* were defiantly setting an example to the *peones, campesinos* and *rancheros* in other parts of Morelos, and elsewhere in southern Mexico. Indeed, conflicts had already broken out, under Francisco Madero and 'Pancho' Villa in the north of the country. The Anencuilco-Ayala insurrection was, so far, quite a small affair; but it was soon to take on national significance. The *Zapatista* and *Maderista* movements, though their aims and ideas were not the same, coincided and, to some extent, helped each other.

IN 1871, Benito Juarez, Mexico's 'greatest president,' stirred up considerable opposition by seeking re-election for a fourth term of office. He was opposed not only by his old friend and vice-President, Sebastien Lerdo de Tejada, but also by General Don Porfirio Diaz, a *mestizo* who had, it was said, fought bravely against the French. In the election, which Diaz claimed had been rigged, no candidate received a clear majority, so, in accordance with the constitution, the Chamber of Deputies had to decide who was to be President. Naturally, they chose Juarez and made Lerdo president of the Supreme Court.

By the spring of the following year, Juarez was, once again, in complete control, of the country; but in the July he died of a heart attack. Sebastien Lerdo automatically succeeded him to the presidency. However, when he too sought re-election in 1876, Diaz sought and obtained the support of a number of Lerdo's political enemies under the banner of 'Effective Suffrage and No Re-election,' and he rebelled. His followers numbered 12,000 men against Lerdo's force of less than 4,000. After some initial reverses, Diaz triumphed, and on November 21, 1876, Don Porfirio rode into Mexico City – and on into the National Palace. New 'elections' gave him the presidency. He then persuaded Congress to reform the constitution, making it illegal for anyone to seek re-election for two successive terms. But Diaz knew what he was doing.

He immediately set himself the task of stabilising the government and of pacifying the country; but, even more importantly, he consolidated his political position, playing off his enemies against each other, and distributing favours to his friends.

When in November, 1880, Diaz's term of office ended, his popularity had almost disappeared. Under the new constitution, he could not stand again for President anyway, but he was able to arrange the 'election' of his trusted friend, General Manuel Gonzalez, the Minister of War. Gonzalez's term of office was 'distinguished' by corruption, graft, scandals and the looting of the Exchequer unequalled even by Mexican standards. By 1884, when the next presidential elections came along, the country had long forgotten Diaz's cry of 'No Re-election.' Diaz was back in office – and he meant to stay there. He forced through Congress a new amendment authorising a second presidential term, and in 1890, a further amendment made it possible for him to remain President for life. Mexico had gotten itself another dictator.

Indeed, that Diaz soon became an absolute ruler very few denied. But Don Porfirio did attempt to tackle the country's parlous economic situation. He cut civil service salaries, cancelled the mortgages on government property and consolidated the internal debt.

As time went by, however, large numbers of former army officers, unemployed since the war with France, were attracted to the Diaz regime by its apparent stability; and large numbers of civilians, most of whom were *mestizos* like Diaz himself, became employees of his ever-expanding bureaucracy. Almost all the state governors became instruments of his dictatorship. And they too were re-elected almost as often as Diaz, whilst many others merely transmitted the succession to their relatives. As a reward for loyalty to the regime, they were also allowed to liquidate political opponents, become owners of *haciendas* and large plantations, organise liquor monopolies and run illegal gambling houses.

The Church hierarchy was mainly concerned in preventing the strict enforcement of the country's anti-clerical laws, and any further confiscation of its immense wealth. Diaz made it quite clear that, whilst leaving such laws on the statute books as a reminder to the Church not to interfere, he would not enforce them. The hierarchy understood and, therefore, kept out of politics other than to give Don Porfirio the Church's blessing.

The press was not forgotten. Soon after Diaz's re-election in 1884, he took it in hand. He summoned all the country's leading journalists to a little 'talk.' During his peroration, he turned the conversation round to the new methods being introduced into Mexico for capital punishment. He casually mentioned the electric chair. They took the hint. Indeed, up to 1900, most newspapers were subsidised by the state. A few papers, such as Ricardo Flores Magon's *Regeneracion*, were published and printed in the United States, and then smuggled into Mexico. Only about twenty per cent of the population could read anyway . . . .

The dictator's control over the judiciary was almost absolute. According to the constitution, subordinate magistrates had to be appointed by the Supreme Court, whilst the Court itself was supposed to be elected by popular vote; but Don Porfirio appointed and removed judges and magistrates at will. Only pro-Diaz lawyers won their cases. And government favourites rarely needed to fear the law. For the *peones, rancheros* and workers, justice was largely non-existent.

The Mexican Federal Army was mainly recruited by forced levies. So-called criminals, which often meant those who had upset the local *jefes politico*, were more often than not given the opportunity, when caught, of choosing between being drafted into the army or being shot. Other 'criminals' were transported to Quitana Roo or the Valle Nacional in Oaxaca, where they were sold as slaves to the local *hacendados* and plantation owners, and made to toil in chain gangs from dawn to dusk under the fierce tropical sun. Most died within a year.

Enterprising bandits and real hold-up men, when caught, were given a different choice. They were recruited into the *Guardia Rurale*, a force somewhat similar to the Spanish *Guardia Civil*. Diaz's *rurales*, moreover, got a good — and legal — living off the Mexican countryside. They wore smart suits of grey or brown suede, with silver embroidery on the jackets and trousers, broad felt hats, red ties — and, of course, large badges of authority. Silver glinted from their horses' saddles; and with their Mauser rifles, revolvers, swords, knives and lassoos they were indeed mobile arsenals. In many areas of the country they terrorised the *peones* and *campesinos*. And by custom of the *ley fuga* they were allowed to shoot their prisoners, explaining afterwards that the unfortunate prisoners had been killed while attempting to escape. There were over 10,000 cases of *ley fuga* killings by *rurales* during Don Porfirio's dictatorship.

The Mexican Indians, throughout the Diaz dictatorship, existed for the most part in a condition of brutish misery, unmatched by the peasants or workers of any other country. Indeed, the much-observed sadness of the Indians was the result of a scant and deficient diet based on corn, *chiles* and *frijoles*. Even their *pulque*, with its high alcohol content, did not help. Indians starved on the central plateau of Anauc where, before the coming of the Spaniards, the Aztecs, Toltecs and Mayans had enjoyed a regime of plenty.

BUT under Diaz Mexico underwent a profound change. Don Porfirio encouraged the flow of foreign capital into the country at particularly advantageous rates of interest. Money poured in from the United States, Britain and elsewhere. Vast sums were invested in the construction of railroads, the mining of silver, and after 1900, oil extraction and the production of coffee, sisal and sugar. Between 1880 and 1890, foreign capital outpaced Mexican investment. Industrial production rose at an annual rate of three-and-a-half per cent between 1878 and 1910. Many public works were undertaken, including major harbours, canals, drainage works and telephone and telegraph lines. A new industrial proletariat was recruited from the former peasants displaced from the land.

Naturally, emphasis on industrialisation increased the already clear-

27

ly defined differences between rich and poor. Industrial capitalism was very largely super-imposed upon the *hacienda* system, under which nearly half of the rural population was bound by debt-*peonage*. Modern capitalism was developing within the shell of a bureaucratic, corrupt and decadent feudalism which had been imposed on Mexico centuries before by Imperial Spain.

In co-operation with foreign interests, Mexico's economy was tightly controlled by a small group of businessmen and financiers, who dominated the money and credit market. In the last decade of the century, a few of them banded together into a group which soon came to be called *cientificos*, because they argued that politics should be a science.

The *cientificos* were extreme partisans of government control by an upper class elite — which, in effect, meant themselves. They argued that Mexico should be ruled by a dictatorship in order to protect the nation against the dangers of political action by the 'illiterate masses,' and from 'anarchy.' In their formative years, however, a few of them contended that a limited democracy, based upon suffrage of the upper class alone, was necessary. But by 1901, one of their number, the Minister of Hacienda, Jose Ives Limantour, devoted all his efforts to guaranteeing that the *cientificos*' control of government affairs would remain absolute after the death of the then ageing Diaz. Ostensibly, the *cientificos* gave unstinted support to the President; in private, they strongly objected to some of his actions. Nevertheless, concerned with their own privileged economic positions, they kept very quiet. Limantour and the *cientificos* took most of the credit for Mexico's economic development — while the economy appeared sound.

But by 1904, there was evidence, tenuous at first, of economic instability.

Following the money panic in the United States, in 1907, the Mexican banks, including the Banco Central Mexicano, though outwardly prosperous, demonstrated symptoms of this instability. They started indulging in speculation, and lending large sums of money on poor security; and institutions authorised to issue bank notes were particularly at fault in over-issuing. Not surprisingly, between 1907 and 1910, inflation was rampant. Such a situation naturally affected the rural poor and, to even a greater extent, the workers of the towns and cities. Between 1893 and 1907, the price of corn – a basic part of the diet of over eighty-five per cent of the population – increased more than fifty per cent. And after 1907, many staple commodities, including cotton, fluctuated in price by as much as four hundred per cent within a period of days. Many *peones* could not even afford to buy up material to make into clothing.

Yet during this period, there was no ascertainable rise in wages. At the beginning of the nineteenth century, average wages were around twenty-five centavos a day; in 1891 they were between twenty-five and fifty, and in 1908 they were back to about twenty-five again. Furthermore, it has been estimated that a day's labour in 1908 only bought one-third as much as it did in 1808. Under such conditions the workers were almost helpless. Their numbers had, of course, increased quite considerably. By 1907, there were 100,000 miners, and around 40,000 textile workers; there were also many tens of thousands of building and railroad workers. But trades unions were practically unknown before 1900; and even if the workers had attempted to organise themselves into unions, they would have found it almost impossible to act on their own behalf. In most of the states of Mexico, laws forbade strikes, and even in the so-called enlightened Federal District heavy fines and imprisonment could be imposed on anyone attempting to 'use physical force' for the purpose of increasing salaries or wages.

Nevertheless, mutual aid and friendly societies were formed, and in 1870 an embryonic trades union centre, called the *Gran Circulo de Obreros*, was also formed. And a few small syndicates were formed through the inspiration of some 'radical' priests.

But many Spanish immigrant workers brought new ideas to Mexico. Anarchist, socialist and syndicalist propaganda began, though on a limited scale, just before the turn of the century. Radical and socialist journals found their way into the country. The most influential of them all was *Regeneracion*, published by the Partido Liberal Mexicano, which, by 1906, had moved so far to the left that it was, to all intents and purposes, an anarchist-communist organisation. Its leaders, the Flores Magon brothers, had been forced to flee the country, but continued to 'direct operations' against the Diaz dictatorship from just across the border in the United States. In 1906, the first industrial conflict broke out at Cananea,

Francisco Madero

Villistas hanged by General Murguia who thought them 'not worth a bullet'.

in the State of Sonora. There was a strike at the American-owned Green Consolidated Mining Company. Following a demonstration, many strikers were shot dead, and the workers were forced back to work under the same conditions. But the workers of Mexico had, at least, begun to move. Other strikes, in the textile industry, followed in 1908 and 1909.

Without quite realising it himself, Don Porfirio began to lose more and more support, except from the few who profited directly, or still hoped to profit, from his rule. Middle-class *mestizos*, and even some *creoles*, also began to strain against the *Porfirista* bureaucracy. Many merchants and industrialists found their markets limited by the poverty of the masses, in both the cities and the countryside. Of course, many of those who turned against the President, or at least no longer gave him active support, did not do so because they opposed his repressive measures in principle, but because they considered that he was becoming old and weak, and that he and his regime could no longer serve their interests. Such men, including some of the great *hacendados* and financiers, were quite willing to see Diaz removed from office, though they looked with horror at the possibility of social reform or, even worse, social revolution.

But violent change was soon to come to Mexico . . . . .

CHAPTER III

MADERO

FRANCISCO Indalecio Madero, born in Parra in the State of Coahuila, on October 30, 1873, was the eldest of two sons of one of the greatest *creole* landowners in northern Mexico.

The Madero family were all engaged in ranching, farming and commerce. None had suffered under Diaz; indeed, their businesses had prospered, and they had all become very rich. It seemed, therefore, quite strange that Francisco Madero should emerge as the catalyst of political and social change. In effect, however, he represented the interests, and forces, not of the old *hacendados* or even the 'plantation capitalists' of states such as Morelos, but of an emergent and developing 'liberal', national bourgeoisie.

Madero soon became convinced that Mexico could only achieve her salvation through universal education. He developed a passion for schools. He also began to take an interest in the conditions and problems of the local *hacienda* workers. Yet despite his interest in material progress, Don Francisco began to dabble in spiritualism. In a way, his spiritualism was a reaction against the crude, vulgar, and ostentatious materialism of the *cientificos* and, particularly, the fun-loving *hacendados*. He was also something of a puritan.

In 1904, Madero started a political reform movement. He founded the Club Democraticio Benito Juarez, and was elected its first president. And in 1908, Madero began to write a book, which appeared in January 1909, as *The Presidential Succession of 1910*. In it he did not mention Diaz by name, but he did mildly criticise his regime. It was a not very well-written book, though it did emphasise the need for universal suffrage and the ending of re-election. Only 3000 copies were sold, but many literate Mexicans read the book. In May 1909, Madero formed the Anti-Re-electionist Party with the slogan: 'Effective Suffrage and No Re-election!'

But even at this stage, Francisco Madero was not personally prepared to challenge Diaz at the polls. Indeed, no one was prepared to challenge Don Porfirio over the presidency. The issue, therefore, revolved around the vice-presidency. Madero was adopted as vice-presidential candidate for the Anti-Re-electionist Party. He had already spoken at a number of meetings, at which he had criticised the dictatorship in general terms – and he had had some of his meetings broken up by *Porfirista* supporters for his pains.

The presidential election was to be on June 26, 1910. Things remained fairly quiet until early June. Then Diaz struck. Madero arrived in Monterrey with Roque Estrada, a member of his party. A meeting had been arranged. But a large crowd of sympathisers, which had assembled at the local railroad station, was violently dispersed by Federals and *rurales*. Madero was allowed to make a short speech to his supporters; but when Estrada attempted to speak, he was ordered not to. He defied the authorities and spoke. Next morning, he was arrested. Madero insisted on seeing the arresting officer's credentials, and in the ensuing argument, Estrada escaped. Madero was immediately arrested and accused of helping Estrada to escape.

On hearing of Madero's arrest, Estrada gave himself up; but on June 21, both were taken to San Luis Potosi and charged with incitement to rebellion. However, ten days previously, Diaz had instructed the Electoral College to announce that the 'election' — which had not even taken place! — had resulted in his re-election. Madero, according to the Electoral College, had received the grand total for the entire country of 196 votes — less than the number of delegates to his party's recent convention! Of course, the Anti-Re-electionist Party complained that the 'election' had been — as usual — a complete farce, but this was rejected by Diaz.

In September, Mexico celebrated, at enormous expense, her Centenary of Independence. Madero and the 'election' were already forgotten.

Francisco Madero, however, at last realised that Don Porfirio Diaz could only be removed by force. So, very reluctantly, he decided to organise an insurrection. On October 6, disguised as a railroad worker, he escaped to Texas. And, there, he proclaimed himself president of a revolutionary junta.

On November 19, Madero left San Antonio in Texas for the Mexican border city of Ciudad, which he felt would be easy to capture with his small army which he had arranged to meet. After crossing the Rio Grande during the night, he found to his disappointment that his army had not turned up, and that the arms and ammunition, for which he had already paid, had not been delivered either. Depressed, he quickly returned to the safety of American soil.

But in Mexico itself things were beginning to move. Some of Madero's supporters had, in fact, acted without their 'leader.' Pascual had easily captured Guerrero, whilst Doroteo Arango — later to be known as 'Pancho' Villa — had captured San Andres. Jose Maria Maytorena, in Sonora, began a movement in that state which soon grew into a series of insurrections. Zacatecas was the scene of a number of unorganised rebellions; but attempts to start insur-rections along the Mexican-Texas border met with very little success. Madero's 'revolution' appeared to be a failure. The New Year showed little evidence of a nation-wide upheaval, though 'Pancho' Villa and a few others continued their resistance in the north of the country. But the movement against Diaz was, in fact, far from moribund. The majority of the population of Mexico City was known to be sympathetic towards the *Maderistas*. And somewhat desultory fighting between Madero's supporters and the Federal Army continued throughout January 1911.

ON March 17, Don Porfirio suspended the Constitution. Jose Limantour, the *cientifico* Minister of Hacienda, arrived in New York, and immediately had unofficial discussions with Madero's brother, Gustavo. Limantour at least recognised that, unless the government instituted a number of reforms, some kind of revolution was inevitable. The aged dictator, however, still did not believe that Madero would succeed. Nevertheless, at the end of March, Diaz's entire Cabinet, except for Limantour and Manuel Gonzalez Cosio, resigned. A new Cabinet was sworn in the same day; but it was no more liberal than the previous one.

Too late, Diaz at least dimly recognised the gravity of the situation. In his message to Congress on April 1, Don Porfirio outlined a reform programme, which included provisions for the correction or elimination of local political and judicial abuses, electoral reform, the election of judges and, even more surprising, limited land reform. In essence, his speech was an admission of his own corruption, maladministration and inefficiency. Moreover, it was an admission of weakness. Madero and his supporters sensed this. Now, nothing less than Diaz's resignation would satisfy them. And every day there were more signs of their eventual success.

At the beginning of April, posters appeared on walls in the capital demanding Diaz's immediate resignation. Ramon Corral, the Vice-President, now seriously ill with cancer, fled on April 12, to Paris. But Diaz was in an even weaker position than he realised. Armed activity against his regime was increasing at an alarming rate. By the beginning of April, the *Maderistas* had occupied a considerable area of the country north of Mexico City. At the end of March, Chilapa, in Guerrero, fell to an armed group led by the Figueroa brothers. On April 15, Acapulco on the Pacific Coast was captured by another group. Veracruz on the East Coast was threatened and, a few days later, *Maderista* forces were operating within sight of Mexico City itself. By May 10, the important city of Ciudad

Juarez was taken by the rebels.

Meanwhile, President Diaz went once again to the Chamber of Deputies, and told them that he would resign 'when, according to the dictates of my conscience, I am assured that my resignation will not be followed by anarchy.' He called on the insurrectionists to lay down their arms. But it was all too late.

On May 17, Diaz, tired and stricken with a jaw infection, succumbed to the inevitable, and was persuaded to resign before the end of the month. Madero sent him a cable congratulating him on his acceptance of the situation, and made arrangements for a general armistice. At ten o'clock on the night of May 21, on the outskirts of Ciudad Juarez, the official peace agreement was signed at a table illuminated by automobile headlights. News of the treaty reached Mexico City on May 23. Demonstrations broke out. Students roamed the streets. And, later, crowds converged on the Zocalo. By early evening the great plaza was jammed with 100,000 people. But even at that late hour, the *Porfirista* dictatorship was not prepared to give in without bloodshed. Federal troops, who had placed themselves on the roofs of the National Palace and the cathedral, began firing at the crowd with rifles and machine-guns just before ten o'clock. For five minutes the Maxims directed their fire full into the crowd. In a few minutes, the plaza was empty except for the dead and wounded. The heavens opened up; and the rains poured down. About 250 had been killed and over 1,000 wounded.

Diaz finally gave in on May 25. Shortly after midnight, Don Porfirio Diaz left the Presidential Palace. Three trains conveyed him, his few remaining followers and members of his family to Veracruz. On the way, bandits attacked the train, but it reached its destination. On May 31, a weeping Don Porfirio boarded a German steamer. And just before leaving for exile, Diaz remarked: 'Madero has unleashed a tiger; let us see if he can control it.' In fact, Madero had unleashed many tigers, the most tenacious of all being Emiliano Zapata – the Man from Morelos.

UNTIL December, 1910, Zapata took very little interest in Madero's campaign. But in January, 1911, he began to attend meetings in the home of a well-known *Maderista* shopkeeper, Pablo Torres Burgos, the 'little ink pot.' A number of other people, including the Puebla chief, Magerito Martinez, Catarino Perdomo from San Pablo Hidalgo, and the very impetuous, but elderly, village chief, Gabriel Tepepa, also attended. The nominal leader, however, was Torres Burgos, because he, to use a phrase, 'knew how to talk.' Early in December, the group sent him to San Antonio to confer with Madero. But the weeks passed, and Torres Burgos did not return.

While he was away, the real *caudillo* of the group was Emiliano Zapata, now president of the enlarged Joint Anencuilco-Ayala-Moyotepec Defence Committee. Zapata had read Madero's proclamations, and had seen the occasional copy of Flores Magon's *Regeneracion*. It was to him that many of the others turned for guidance on future activity. Some of them were unable to decide whether to let the planters and *hacendados* stockpile arms and mobilise, or to rebel immediately. Some intended to act at once. Cautious as always, Zapata exerted all his strength of persuasion to keep them from taking premature action. He urged them to wait for the return of Torres Burgos, who had by then been away for almost six weeks. But he was not entirely successful.

'Pretend peaceableness,' said Zapata. 'Let the garrisons slowly be sucked away to meet uprisings two thousand kilometres off. Then, make a quick pounce. Annihilate weakened garrisons, and then seize the state and make a feint in force, if not an outright attack on Mexico City. That will strike right at the heart of our enemies, upset all their plans of defence and throw them into confusion and panic. But wait . . . .'

Stubbornly he held his hand. At the same time, however, he quietly made plans for mobilising and recruiting his forces. Indeed by the beginning of March, there were already around 3,000 *insurrectos* mobilised in Morelos and the adjoining states of Puebla and Guerrero. But there was a chronic shortage of both guns and ammunition. Emiliano Zapata had a .44 calibre Winchester, as well as two colts, but most of the *insurrectos* still had only their *machetes* slung in leather scabbards alongside their saddles. Nevertheless, the Liberation Army of the South and Centre -- as it was later to be called -- was beginning to take shape. And its nucleus -- sometimes called by its enemies the 'Death Legion' -- was to remain with Zapata, first at Villa de Ayala, and, afterwards, at various hideouts in Morelos and Puebla. Its banner was crimson, featuring 'Our Lady of Mercy the Virgin of Guadalupe' (the dark Virgin) surmounted on a black skull-and-cross-bones!

On February 7, old Gabriel Tepepa rebelled at Tlaquiltenango. The restless old man, together with a few 'young bloods', headed north and two days later took Tepoztlan. They destroyed the municipal archives, and ransacked the house of the local *jefe politico*. And then they disappeared into the hills. A few days later, they attacked the state capital of Cuernevaca, but were easily routed by a detachment of the Federal Army Ninth Cavalry which was garrisoned there. Tepepa and his group once again fell upon Tlaquiltenango, hanged the *jefe*, seized the Post Office, looted a number of stores and, as before, fled before a rapidly advancing force of Federals up into the mountains.

And still Zapata waited.

He would not move. It was harvest time. The planters began to demand extra protection for their ripe cane and, even more important, for their expensive machinery. On March 8, Governor Escandon ordered the reorganisation and expansion of the state's *rurales*. Now, it was time to act. Torres Burgos had just returned from San Antonio with a copy of Madero's *Plan*, but little advice and no promise of assistance from Madero. So, on March 9, Burgos, old Jose Merino and Emiliano Zapata met in Cuautla – and drew up their plans. And during the next morning they sent out messengers. In the night, *Zapatistas* in Villa de Ayala disarmed the local police, and called a general assembly of all the people. Torres Burgos read out Madero's *Plan*; and Otilio Montano, a local schoolteacher, climbed upon a makeshift platform, and shouted: 'Down with the *hacendados*! Long live the *pueblos*! *Viva la revolucion*! and *Viva tierra y libertad*!' Zapata said nothing. But before the first light of morning, he had organised a column of about sixty volunteers. Some of them were only boys of fourteen or fifteen years of age.

During the day, Zapata and his column moved down the Cuautla river where, previously, he had run his string of mules, and on to the *rancho* of Rafael Zaragoza. More men and youths joined them there. They rode south and encamped in the hills. Collecting more volunteers and horses in all the *pueblos* and small *ranchos*, but avoiding the large *haciendas*, they moved across the state line into Puebla.

37

Zapata's Banner.

Their ultimate aim was to capture Cuautla. Torres Burgos gave the orders, but Emiliano Zapata worked out the strategy. And he knew that his ill-armed and untried warriors would be incapable of capturing Cuautla, or any large town, in a direct battle with Federal troops.

So the *Zapatista* 'horde' continued to move south unmolested. Scouts were sent forward on the gallop to rouse the villagers. And out of the *pueblos, ranchos* and some *haciendas* there poured forth cotton-clad men, youths and boys. Again and again there was the painful task of sorting out the equipped from the unequipped, and the able from the less able. Few of the volunteers had guns. Zapata insisted on at least a mount and a *machete*. His plan was to capture sufficient arms, train the volunteers and then get control of the area below a line from Jojutla to Yecapixtla. Thus, they could slowly control all key points along the Interocean Railroad from Puebla to Cuautla. Caution, careful planning and organisation were all-important if they were to succeed.

RIGHT from the onset of the campaign, Zapata displayed both courage and ingenuity. In one of the very first engagements, he commandered a locomotive, loaded it with men, drove it on to the narrow gauge tracks that connected a number of *haciendas*, and crashed it through the gates of the Hacienda de Huichila, to seize rifles, ammunition and horses. Considerable care, however, had to be taken by *Zapatistas* not to be captured alive by the *rurales* or Federals. For they were quite merciless. They would hang a prisoner, and then while he hung there they would light a fire under him, and roast him to death. As time went by, the *Zapatistas* and other insurrectionists began to retaliate. It was soon to become a cruel and bitter struggle.

Quite early on a crisis developed among the Morelos rebels, largely through the activities of the impetuous Gabriel Tepepa and his 'young bloods.' Tepepa had left the hills, and had joined up with the main body of the *insurrectos*. He and his young warriors were full of confidence, and were eager to attack Jojutla and possibly Jonacatepec. Rumour had it that Jonacatepec was lightly held. Torres Burgos, therefore, decided that the time had come to make an all-out attack on Jojutla. Zapata disagreed but was, on that occasion, over-ruled. Burgos elaborated his plan. Rafael Merino, Jose's son, was to carry out a diversionary attack on Jonacatepec; Zapata was to patrol the Puebla-Morelos state line, and Burgos was to lead Tepepa's warriors against Jojutla.

On March 22, the state governor, Escandon, having heard of the proposed attack on Jojutla, left the state capital, Cuernavaca, with a group of the Federal Army Ninth Cavalry and a few *rurales*. Two days later, however, Torres Burgos rode into Tlaquiltenango about ten kilometres to the north. Thereupon, Escandon took fright and headed back to Cuernavaca as fast as his horse would take him, followed by the Federals and the *rurales*, the local police and town officials. Meanwhile, Zapata and his 'Death Legion' deliberately decided to attack Jonacatepec against the 'orders' of Torres Burgos and Gabriel Tepepa. It was a cross-country trek of some eighty kilometres over rolling *llano*, far from the railway line. Zapata opened his attack just before dawn with a half-moon of fire from small groups widely spaced among the surrounding hills. But he soon found his positions raked by rifle fire and later, machine-gun fire. Jonacatepec was not as lightly held as was thought. Emiliano and his men immediately withdrew. On the other hand, Burgos with Tepepa's forces swept into Jojutla, where they began looting stores and business premises. Burgos was horrified. Instructions had been given forbidding indiscriminate looting; such activity was not in line with the objectives of the Morelos movement. Burgos, therefore, summoned Zapata and old Merino to Jojutla, and informed them and the other chiefs that he had decided to resign. And, together with his two sons, he started to return to Villa de Ayala. The following day, however, the three of them were ambushed by a small force of Federals, captured and executed on the spot. The Morelos rebels' first real campaign was largely a failure.

The Morelenses, moreover, now had no supreme chief; no *caudillo*. There was considerable confusion at first. Returning to Puebla, many of the chiefs and 'revolutionary colonels', as they were beginning to be called, assembled and discussed the situation and, after much deliberation, elected Emiliano Zapata as 'Supreme Chief of the Revolutionary Movement of the South.' He became General Zapata of the Liberation Army of the South and Centre.

The Morelos revolutionaries seemed to have learnt their lesson.

During the attack on Jonacatepec, Zapata's horse, Pavon, was shot through the lungs and had to be destroyed. Zapata was naturally heartbroken. But the news soon reached the priest, Father Morentin, a lonely scholar, and a disciple of Fourrier and Saint Simon and a supporter of the *insurrectos*. He had recently inherited his brother's small *rancho* and a few horses. He immediately presented Emiliano Zapata with a young dappled-grey stallion dubbed, for its speed, Relampago.

CHAPTER IV

MORELOS ON THE MOVE

LATE IN March, 1911, Emiliano Zapata met Octavio Magana, an independent *Maderista*, and asked him to inform Francisco Madero and the *Maderistas* in Mexico City that he – Zapata – had been provisionally elected supreme chief of the revolutionaries in Morelos and the South, following the death of Torres Burgos. No reply came, as many of Magana's group in the capital had been arrested. Zapata's somewhat tenuous connections with Madero were, nonetheless, soon to be established.

In Morelos and the South, new chiefs and their men joined the Liberation Army daily. There was Francisco Mendoza, a *ranchero* from just across the Puebla state line; there was Jesus 'One-Eye' Morales, a saloon barkeeper from Ayutla, and Felipe Neri, a kiln operator from Chinameca, and Gordino Ayaquica, a textile worker from Atlixco . . . and many others. There was even a renegade protestant preacher, Jose Trinidad Ruiz, from Tlaltizapan. And each had between fifty and two hundred men -- and some women, the *Zapatistas'* famous, or infamous, *soldaderas* who accompanied the men everywhere and often fought alongside them. At about the same time, Zapata also welcomed a few radical and libertarian 'intellectuals' into his camp to help organise and, as he remarked to Otilio Montano at the time, 'put some order into these people – the chiefs – for whom, once the fight begins, there is no god who can hold them back.'

41

Meanwhile, small groups of *Magonista insurrectos* were fighting in Baja California, Chihuahua, Sonora and Veracruz, completely independent of the *Maderistas*, and isolated from the *Zapatistas*, over 2,000 kilometres to the south.

In Veracruz and Baja California, in particular, the idea of *communismo libertario* had taken root; but early on in the *Magonista* campaign, one of Ricardo Flores Magon's closest collaborators, the young poet, Praxedis Guerrero, had been killed in a raid on the small Chihuahua town of Janos. Also, a few of the *Magonistas* went over to Madero; and though the *Magonistas* for a short while controlled the northern part of Baja California — establishing their own anarchist commune or republic in the desert! — they remained completely isolated not only from the main body of *Maderistas* but, far more important, from the *Zapatista* insurrection as well, mainly due to the geographical isolation of the Californian peninsula. Nevertheless, their ideas and ideals, together with Flores Magon's slogan, '*tierra y libertad!*' were accepted in varying degrees by Zapata and a few of his comrades. The *Magonista* objective of common ownership of the land had, of course, always been part and parcel *Zapatismo* and the *peone* movement of Morelos and the South.

Following Zapata's election as Supreme Chief, his brother Eufemio, returned from his wanderings, and joined Emiliano in Jonacatepec. But there were still a few village chiefs in Morelos, and the four influential Figueroa brothers in Guerrero, who did not accept Emiliano Zapata as commander-in-chief of all the *insurrectos* of the South. In the central areas, the forces of Montano, Neri and Salazar accepted him; and to the west and south of Cuernavaca, Genovevo de la O's *guerrilleros*, though independent, also co-operated with the *Zapatistas*. But in other areas of southern Morelos, rebel chiefs such as the Miranda brothers, sided with the Figueroa brothers. And the Figueroa brothers were formidable rivals. Nevertheless, Zapata decided that, despite his suspicions of the affluent brothers, co-operation with them would be the best policy. So Ambrosio Figueroa and Emiliano Zapata met at Jolapan, in 'neutral' Puebla, on April 22, 1911, and worked out an agreement: Zapata was accepted as nominal Supreme Chief of the Liberation Army of the South, while the Figueroa brothers' forces would operate freely in any part of the South outside the state of Morelos. When joint operations were to take place in Morelos, then Zapata would be chief; and when joint operations were to take place in Guerrero, then Ambrosio Figueroa would be chief. But the Figueroa brothers had no intention of keeping the agreement. Indeed, they were soon to break it.

It was agreed that the *Zapatistas*, now over 3,000 strong, and the *Figueroaistas* would jointly attack and, this time, capture and hold Jojutla by the end of April. It was already the second week of the month, and the snows were melting, the rains were beginning and the rivers of Morelos were rising. It would be a long ride across mountains, valleys and desert; but Jojutla had to be captured – and captured quickly. And then Zapata received disquieting news. A messenger, Felipe Casales, reported:

'*Mi general,* the Guerrenese *gente* have camped close to Jojutla for two weeks now . . . but they have done nothing . . . they have plenty to eat . . . plenty to drink . . . no one has fired a shot . . . and General Beltran has a good force of Federals, many men, many guns, machine-guns and cannons . . . they tell me that General Figueroa and General Beltran are old friends, very good friends . . . and they have made an agreement not to fight each other.'

'And,' he continued, 'the Figueroa brothers intend to assassinate you, *mi general.'*

Emiliano Zapata believed him.

In an ugly mood, Zapata, with the Liberation Army, moved not south towards Jojutla, but away from it, on a long march to Zacualpan. Then, Zapata returned to Villa de Ayala – and waited. Two weeks later, a junta of about thirty Morelos chiefs met at Jantetelco, and worked out their strategy. First, they would take Yautepec, and then Cuautla. They would have no truck with dubious allies.

Harry H. Dunn, an American journalist who worked for the International News Service and claimed to have accompanied Zapata on the campaign, describes the attack on Yautepec.

'Early one dry morning, we rode out of Villa de Ayala, Emiliano in the lead, Eufemio in the rear, between them the thousand men of the 'Death Legion' . . . We passed through half-a-dozen small towns, and as many villages . . . And about mid-afternoon of the next day we rode over a range of low hills to look down on Yautepec, thousand year-old outpost of the Nahua Empire against the Guerrero and Zapotec nations . . . .

Zapata sent three men to demand the surrender of Colonel Romulo Yanes and the two companies of Federal soldiers – about two-hundred-and-forty men – in the *cuartel* of Yautepec. These returned immediately with the defiant refusal of the old officer, who had fought Indians under Porfirio Diaz forty years before. The 'horde' settled into a ring around Yautepec.

The guard at the door of the barracks was changed. The Mexican tricolour floated upward to its daytime place at the top of the staff. Smoke of cooking-fires rose from the *corral* at the rear of the *cuartel*. The military arm was awake, but the streets and the plaza remained deserted. Not a shop opened its doors or took down the heavy shutters from its windows. An officer came out of the *cuartel*, looked up and down the street, went inside, leaving the great door ten feet wide and a foot thick, standing open. Two soldiers, bayonets fixed, guarded the entrance.

Seven small boys, fourteen or fifteen years old, loitered in the plaza. Chasing each other, they crossed this little park, and began playing in the wide street in front of the barracks. All of them lit long black cigars from one match. They spread out, one remaining before the open door, three on each side, running or playing leap-frog away from him. The guards watched idly.

Suddenly, the little fellows reached inside their ragged shirts. They withdrew small, round, bright objects, tin cans, with a short piece of string dangling from each. The boys touched these strings to the burning ends of their cigars, then hurled the round, bright objects at the *cuartel.* Two threw their cans on the tiled roof. Four pitched them into the narrow windows, from which the muzzles of machine-guns peered. The boy at the centre threw his toy into the open door. All ran, each in any direction he chose, away from the barracks.

A section of the roof rose in the air. The great door leaned forward, split down the centre, and fell. The two guards disappeared. One second they were leaning on their rifles; the next they were gone, obliterated in a heart-beat. Fragments of other men came through the gaping doorway. A machine-gun lifted up, pitched forward and, held fast by its breech-mechanism, tipped out of the window.

44

A smothered thump, as if someone had smitten a muted drumhead, shook the shutters. Three men reeled out of a doorway, staggered about, and fell. They never rose. A head came through a window, bounced, rolled across the road and into the plaza. The boy who hurled his bomb through the door lay sprawled, like a discarded doll, in the street. The six others seem to have escaped . . . . the "horde" swept into the plaza.

The Federals, half their number dead or wounded, and the others smothered in the fumes of dynamite, fought desperately, hand in hand, bayonet against *machete*. Eventually, the long knives, known to their Indian wielders from boyhood, won the battle.

In less than an hour the fighting ceased. Zapata, with one of his officers, appeared in a doorway. Hands bound, head up, the white-haired commander of the Federals followed, surrounded by a score of *Zapatistas*. Emiliano led the way to a nearby wall. This happened to be the side of the principle church of Yautepec. Colonel Yanes was backed against it. A member of the "Death Legion" offered to bind his eyes, but the veteran refused. A priest, defying death, stepped from the church door, and held a cross aloft, so that the doomed man might see it. Above the rattle and shouts of command rose a brave man's prayer for the soul of another.

Five *Zapatistas* moved back, ten feet from the wall. They levelled their carbines. Emiliano's *machete* rose and fell. Over the crackling volley of the Mausers sang the farewell of their victim to life: *'Viva Mejico! Viva Diaz!'*

The ordinary Federal soldiers, most of whom were conscripts, were offered the choice of joining the *Zapatistas* or making their way home. About fifty joined. The officers, unless found guilty of cruelty to the civilian population, were made to take an oath that they would not bear arms against the revolution again, and also sent on their way. Some were even given a few day's rations. Two or three, like Colonel Yanes, were executed. Such was to be the usual *Zapatista* policy regarding prisoners-of-war.

FOLLOWING the capture of Yautepec and the defeat of the Federal garrison at Jonactepec, Zapata and the Liberation Army moved north – behind Cuautla – raiding the towns of Atlixco and Metepec, collecting ammunition, arms and provisions. News came of the *Maderistas'* capture of Ciudad Juarez on the Texas border. Zapata camped at Yecapixla, and made preparations for the attack on Cuautla, fifty kilometres to the north. It was to be a long and bloody campaign.

Zapata called a conference of chiefs. He spoke quietly, unemotionally, yet emphatically.

'We have 4,000 men, but only 1,000 guns . . . They have the 'Golden Fifth' regiment . . . they are only 400 strong . . . but they are good fighters . . . they are expecting 600 Federal reinforcements commanded by Victoriano Huerta, the old Diaz general, to join them from Cuernavaca. It is going to be a tough battle . . . . '

Huerta's reinforcements did not arrive. Nevertheless, the Federals in Cuautla prepared their defence. Men took up positions on the roofs overlooking the park. All entrances to the town were barricaded. A cannon pointed down the main street. The pattern of attack followed that of Yautepec. First, a number of buildings were dynamited, and then set on fire. *Zapatista* cavalry slowly advanced to about 300 metres from the first barricade, and then charged. They were repulsed. Zapata called on the Federals to surrender; but, as in Yautepec, they refused. Zapata's plan now was continuous attack — twenty-four hours a day, seven days a week if necessary.

Cuautla, like all Mexican *pueblos* of any size, was a natural fortress. Against all but heavy artillery, adobe was almost impregnable; almost as impregnable as masonry. Zapata did all he could to hold his men back, but many went needlessly to their slaughter. Again and again, dynamite was used against the almost impregnable walls. Then, at last Zapata decided to launch a mass attack. Half the town was in flames. The fighting continued for six days, hand-to-hand, in the streets, on the roofs, in the ruins of buildings. Still no reinforcements came. Federal troops defending the north gate, at last, gave in. Zapata had been right when he argued that the government would be forced to deplete the garrisons of Morelos and the South, and send the Federals against Madero and Villa in the north of the country.

The Liberation Army of the South occupied Cuautla, much of which had been gutted. The dead and wounded cluttered the streets.

With the capture of Cuautla, Zapata now had at least one solid base; but the Liberation Army did not control the whole of Morelos or any other southern state, though Zapata and his allies had sufficient control to lay claim to much of the area. Cuernavaca, the Morelos state capital, was still in Federal hands. But at least the victorious Madero would be forced to recognise General Zapata and the Liberation Army of the South and Centre.

Meanwhile, though the capture of such places as Cuautla and Yautepec were the dramatic successes of the Morelos revolutionaries, the raiding of large *haciendas* continued apace. On occupying Cuautla, Zapata and the chiefs sent out a directive to all the *pueblos* and villages in the area to the effect that the *peones* should not hesitate to reclaim their lost *ejidos* and common lands from the *hacendados* and sugar-cane planters. Immediately, *peones* and small *rancheros* began taking over fields in many parts of the central and eastern areas of the state.

Morelos was on the move . . . .

But the forces of reaction were far from beaten. Ambrosio Figueroa had already conferred with 'respectable' *Madersitas* and *jefes* in Mexico City — while Zapata was capturing Yautepec. Now, he was being approached by a number of businessmen, merchants and *hacendados* from Morelos, who appealed to him and his forces in Guerrero to occupy Morelos, and save them from Zapata! At first Figueroa hesitated; then he agreed. He sent about 1,000 men to Cuernavaca to reinforce the Federal garrison. And on May 21, the *Figueroaistas* from Guerrero occupied the Morelos capital. A smaller force also occupied Jojutla. On May 23, Madero asked Zapata by telegram to 'suspend attacks' on the *haciendas* of Calderon, Chinameca and Hospital when, in fact, he was not attacking them.

Despite *Zapatista* successes, the Morelos movement was being hindered and thwarted. The planters were still there, and resisting; the governor, Escandon, was still there; the state legislators, congressmen and *jefes* were still there, and, despite the fact that all of them were Diaz supporters, Zapata and the *peones* were expected to respect their authority until new officials were appointed, presumably by Madero. At the end of May, old Gabriel Tepepa arrived in Jojutla from Cuautla with a few young companions; and on arrival was conveniently murdered by an old enemy, Federico Morales.

Zapata waited. But he would go to Mexico City, and meet

Madero on his arrival.

MADERO's first message to the Mexican people, following the departure of Porfirio Diaz, was a brief explanation of the peace settlement, a renunciation of the provisional presidency, which he had assumed the previous November, and a call for support of the existing presidency of Francisco Leon de la Barra, an old Diaz diplomat, until the new elections at the end of the year.

Francisco Madero then formed his government. Rafael Hernandez, Madero's cousin and an arch-conservative, was appointed Minister of Justice; Ernest Madero was made Minister of Hacienda — another 'liberal' conservative. A number of other people who had taken very little part in the *Maderista* 'revolution' received various posts, but many of Madero's erstwhile supporters were extremely dissatisfied with the appointments. The main bone of contention was over the appointment of so many of Madero's relatives and personal friends to positions of power. Much the same occured over the appointment of state governors. The 'liberal', Francisco Madero, often acted extremely illiberally.

As soon as 'peace' had, however, been restored Madero proceeded to Mexico City. He arrived on June 7; and, despite the misgivings of many, it was indeed a triumphant entry. Over 100,000 people lined the streets to welcome him. Many thousands of *insurrectos* from all over Mexico — complete with their arms! — mingled with the crowds. It was a colourful, noisy and joyful occasion. Among those who met Madero at the station was Emiliano Zapata. But he had more on his mind than mere festivities.

The following day, Zapata went to the Madero family's residence on Berlin Street, and, for the first time, met Francisco in his study. They had much to talk about. First Zapata stressed his mistrust of the affluent Figueroa brothers, but Madero pleaded with him to co-operate with them. Zapata reluctantly agreed. Then, Emiliano told Don Francisco that he did not trust Juan Carreon, the manager of the Bank of Morelos in Cuernavaca, whom Madero had appointed as provisional governor of the state. He expected nothing from a banker. Nor was Zapata prepared to demobilise the Liberation Army of the South until the land question had been settled.

'What concerns us,' explained Zapata, 'is that, right away, the land must be returned to the *pueblos*, to the people . . . and the promises which the revolution made be carried out.'

Carreon, said Zapata, was a banker, operating in collusion with the planters. 'If that happens when the people are armed, what would happen if they disarm?' he asked Madero.

He then stood up, walked over to where Madero was sitting and, pointing his rifle at the gold watch which spread across Don Francisco's waistcoat, asked:

'Senor Madero, if I take advantage of the fact that I am armed and you are not, and take away your watch and keep it, and after a while we meet again, both of us armed the same, would you have the right to demand that I give it back?'

'Certainly,' replied Madero. 'And I would ask for an indemnity.'

'Well,' concluded Zapata, 'that's what has happened in Morelos, where a few planters have taken over our lands. My soldiers – the armed *rancheros* and all the people in the villages – demand that I tell you, will full respect, that they want the restitution of their lands to be got underway right now.'

Zapata was quite adamant.

Madero promised him that he would look into the matter; and he accepted Zapata's invitation to visit Morelos the following Monday, June 12, to see things for himself. It would be his first visit to the state. Madero was much distressed over his interview with Emiliano Zapata. He had never met anyone like him before.

On arrival in Cuernavaca, Madero first met a group of local merchants. Carreon arranged a banquet for him. Madero then met a number of *hacendados* in Iguala; the day after he conferred at length with the Figueroa brothers. At Cuautla, on June 15, he was shown the destruction and the ruined buildings sustained during the *Zapatista* attack. Afterwards he met Zapata in the city. Right at the onset, he offered Zapata a large *hacienda* in the state of Veracruz, and the right to maintain a small personal armed escort, in return for Zapata's withdrawal from the revolutionary scene. Emiliano rejected his offer contemptuously. He explained – for the second time – that he was fighting for the restoration of the people's common lands and *ejidos*, and that he was incapable of selling out to Madero or anyone else. Zapata strode out. Disappointed, Don

Francisco Madero returned to Mexico City, convinced that he was going to have considerable trouble with the Attila of the South, as the yellow press in the capital was calling Zapata. On his arrival in Cuernavaca, Madero had been welcomed with roses and gardenias; pajama-clad, sandal-shod *Zapatistas* had stood respectfully to attention, and *Zapatista* horsemen, trussed in cartridge belts and bristling with sidearms, rifles and *machetes* had rode at his side as a guard of honour. His departure, however, was a different matter. Few bothered to see him off.

Zapata was not happy either. With the victory of the *Maderistas* the various insurgent armies were expected to disband. And the Liberation Army of the South was no exception. The compulsory disarmament of the *Zapatistas* — together with the discharge of over 3,000 men — would be a blow to Zapata, particularly as he had received no specific promises from Madero regarding the land question. And the *hacendados* were still there, even if a few of them had lost some of their fields or had had some of their crops destroyed.

The *Zapatistas* were supposed to hand their arms over on June 13, at the La Carolina factory just north of Cuernavaca. The 'Death Legion' encamped outside the city. They maintained excellent order. Most of them brought three guns — mostly discarded rifles and old muzzle-loading shotguns, often taken from the *haciendas*. Madero's special commissioner, Gabriel Robles Dominguez, arranged for the *Zapatistas* to turn in their arms to a state official at one table, pass on to a second where he and the *Zapatista* chief-of-staff, Abraham Martinez, gave them their discharge papers; and then on to a third table to collect their 'pay' — ten pesos if the man came from around Cuernavaca, fifteen pesos if from farther afield and a bonus for handing in a revolver or pistol as well as a rifle — all of which was in new 'two-face' notes printed on Madero's presses in Mexico City. Altogether, 3,500 arms were handed over, and almost 5,000 pesos paid out. The operation seemed a success.

Nevertheless, though the men from Morelos were, for the most part, simple illiterate *peones* and *rancheros*, they were not stupid. Most of the Mausers and better rifles were not handed in. And Zapata himself was more than a little suspicious of Madero's intentions. He and the 'disbanded' Liberation Army would most probably need those guns again — perhaps quite soon.

To a casual observer the Mexican revolution seemed quite chaotic. and purposeless. Small armies and guerrilla bands appeared to be rushing about in all directions. The whole country seemed to be in a state of disintegration. And Mexico was far from being pacified and united under Francisco Madero. But, as early as June, 1911, a distinct pattern had emerged. In fact, the country was actually rent into three completely irreconcilable camps.

The first group was the old deeply entrenched *hacendado*, land-owning element, supported by the Catholic Church, a few home-grown financiers and a powerful coterie of foreign concessionaires, chiefly American and British. Politically, they were *Porfiristas*. And they were already plotting a new dictatorship, and looking for a new and younger dictator.

The second group was the emergent, rising bourgeoisie – the business, professional and small landowning class, which included a few politically ambitious *hacendados* and affluent *rancheros* like the Figueroa brothers. They were often nationalistic (which meant being anti-American and anti-British) and, like the bourgeoisie of seventeenth-century England and eighteenth-century France, they favoured a somewhat limited constitutional democracy that would liberate them from the fetters of a largely fuedal absolutism, and give them a modern business administration, responsive to their needs. Unconcerned for the mass of the Mexican people, they desired only such improvements in their lot as would weaken the power of the *hacendados* and the Church, and increase the home market for industrial and other consumer goods. Their man was Madero – a typical eighteenth-century bourgeois and 'liberal.'

The third group was the great mass of Mexico's dispossessed – the debt-slaves (the *peones*), the small *rancheros*, sharecroppers and *campesinos*, and the new class of industrial wage-workers: the miners, railroad workers and the like. And like the dispossessed peasants of Britain and France, they too supported, if less enthusiastically, a bourgeois leader. Madero was also their man.

But within the third group there was what might be called a sub-group. Confined almost to Morelos and a few neighbouring states, without intellectual aid save for a few idealists from Mexico City and the *Magonsita* propaganda of *Regeneracion*, it stood apart from the mainstream of events. Yet, in the words of Edcumb

Pinchon, 'this group conquered Morelos without a peso, a cartridge or a gun, save what had been wrested from the enemy, yet it has publicly formulated its demands: the restoration of the communal lands . . . .' These were the *Zapatistas*. But they had not, as yet, 'conquered' Morelos.

CHAPTER V

INTERRUPTED HONEYMOON

BY THE middle of June, Madero had to concern himself with a series of problems. He was criticised for not purging the Federal Army, most of whose officers were Diaz appointees. The appointment of known conservatives to his Cabinet had not made him popular with the radicals. Within a month of his entry into Mexico City, he began to lose support. He, therefore, decided to make a pronouncement. He affirmed his faith in the people's ability to govern themselves 'with serenity and wisdom' and he promised to alleviate the suffering of the 'lower orders.'

But Madero made no promises to raise wages or salaries – except by 'dint of hard work.' He told the 'upper classes' that they could no longer count on the impunity which those privileged by fortune had hitherto enjoyed. And he also promised 'justice according to the law' to everyone. He was conciliatory. Yet he pleased no one. By July, he had fallen out with a number of his 'revolutionary' generals; and he warned them that he would not tolerate their interference in political matters.

Meanwhile, in Morelos, the *hacendados* and some of the old Diaz politicians began to put pressure on Zapata. They even attempted to exclude him from local administrative decision-making. And they informed Madero and the government that he was planning an immediate uprising in the state. In Cuernavaca, a group of *Porfiristas* organised a para-military group – *Los Hijos de Morelos* – to save themselves from Zapata 'the savage,' and Madero 'the little Jewish upstart.' (Though born a Catholic, who later dabbled in Spiritualism, Madero was said to be of Portuguese-Jewish origin; and this was emphasised by reactionary elements). Some of the younger

Morelos *hacendados* banded themselves into an aristocratic *creole* volunteer corps, dubbed *Los Colorados.*

Madero had established absolute freedom of the press. But practically every newspaper in Mexico City was owned by the *hacendado-cientifico* group — and these were the only papers of any consequence in the entire country. The result was that Emiliano Zapata soon found himself the butt of a campaign of vilification almost unequaled in the history of modern journalism. He was called a 'licentious and a savage demon,' 'the modern Attila,' the 'Attila of the South' and worse. The *Zapatistas* were described as wild revolutionary bandits, clad in cotton pyjamas and sandals, who carried razor-sharp *machetes*. Naturally, they were 'swarthy' Indians of an 'inferior race' who, led by Zapata, reeled through Morelos slaughtering rich and poor alike, and committing unspeakable attrocities without end. And Cuernavaca, they proclaimed, was a city without women — all had been raped and then cut to pieces! This was the situation as portrayed by the yellow press.

But Mrs. Rosa E. King, the English proprietress of La Bella Vista, Cuernavaca's famous resort hotel, who had been there throughout the 'troubles,' had not noticed it. Sitting with her teenage daughter in the patio of the hotel, she noted in her diary:

'I simply do not believe it, what the papers say, that the *Zapatistas* who have lived among us for weeks so peaceable have turned overnight into villainous desperados . . . They seem to me like harmless and valiant children more than anything else . . . Rough and untaught as Zapata's followers are, they have treated us with true kindness and consideration during the occupation of the town, and I have come to have confidence in their natural qualities.'

Don Francisco also began to worry. He summoned Emiliano to Mexico City, and told him what he had been reading in the papers. Zapata tried to convince him that what he had read was not true. All that he, Zapata, was interested in was peace, justice and liberty, and the return of the people's lands. Zapata left. And after the meeting, Madero informed the planters, *hacendados*, merchants and *jefes* of Morelos that he had settled the Zapata 'problem.' He was sure that Zapata would retire — probably accept a *hacienda* somewhere — pay off all his men, and accept a new state governor and administration. All the good citizens would then be able, once again, to sleep safely in their beds, and business would continue as before.

But the *hacendados* and planters were not convinced or mollified . . .

Carreon, the state governor, pleaded with Madero's Minister of the Interior, Jesus Flores Magon, the former anarchist and brother of Ricardo, to send more Federal troops to Morelos. For the *Zapatistas* may have demobilised or, at least, partially demobilised, but they were not demoralised; and the villagers around Cuautla were refusing to give up the fields they had taken from the planters earlier in the year. About the same time, a number of village assemblies and their chiefs began to propose Zapata for governor of Morelos. But he refused to even consider the idea. He was not interested in political power. Indeed, he would have been more than happy to have returned to his little *rancho* and settle down. He was, however, still Supreme Chief of the Liberation Army of the South and Centre, even if that body was supposed to have been demobilised. Unfortunately, for General Zapata, events in Puebla forced him to act.

Madero had been invited to visit Puebla City on July 13. He was to deliver an address. There had been the usual rumours of an attempt on Madero's life; and there were still many Diaz supporters among the well-to-do. A number of *Zapatistas*, as well as Zapata's chief-of-staff, Abraham Martinez, were encamped in the city, and in the bullring, together with many women and children. Then, Martinez actually unearthed a serious plot against the life of Madero. The leaders of the plot included the *Porfirista* ex-governor and two state legislators. Martinez arrested them. This was the kind of situation the *Porfiristas* had been waiting for. A gang of them sped through the city in fast cars, deliberately firing pistols at *Zapatista* patrols. The interim President, de la Barra, ordered the arrest of Martinez, who was picked up by local *rurales* and thrown into Puebla jail. During the following night, Federal troops attacked the bullring, and killed eighty and wounded over 200 people, including many of the women and children. Surprisingly, Madero praised the troops 'for restoring order.'

On hearing the news Zapata immediately called upon all the chiefs to mobilise, and assemble at Cuautla for a march on Puebla. Madero was told that Zapata was ready to move. He instructed Zapata to

stay where he was. And he did. But the *Zapatistas* remained mobilised. Madero went to Tehuacan, where he invited Zapata to meet
him. Zapata ignored his request. Madero invited him again. He
still refused. But Madero asked him yet again; and this time Zapata
agreed that his brother, Eufemio, and one of his men, Jesus Morales,
would go and talk with Madero.

Meanwhile, Emiliano Zapata had other matters on his mind.

HE WAS just on thirty-two; and he had, for some while, been courting
a young woman by the name of Josefa, whose father, a horse dealer
whom Emiliano had known, had died early in 1909. Emiliano
Zapata decided to get married. A *contracto de matrimonio* gave a
man a place in his community; it also perpetuated the 'clan' name.
In the past Emiliano's amorous attachments had been numerous and
usually casual; but he had been fond of Josefa longer than anyone
else. His 'honeymoon' however, was to last for just one night.

During the wedding celebrations on August 9, Zapata received
information that General Victoriano Huerta had crossed into Morelos
with 1,000 Federal troops, in order to 'disarm the Southerners if
they were opposed to being discharged.' And the next day, Huerta
and his Federals entered Cuernavaca. Zapata telegraphed a protest
to Madero, and asked: 'Have you any complaints against me?' He
received no reply. On August 11, Governor Carreon called off the
proposed state elections, and General Huerta quartered his infantry
battalion in the state capital. And the day after that, the interim
President, de la Barra, suspended the state's sovereignty, which was
tantamount to declaring martial law in Morelos. Huerta was now
free to begin his campaign against the *Zapatistas*. He would, he
boasted, proceed with the 'annihilation of the rebels.'

De la Barra had already 'bought' the Guerrero *Zapatista* leader,
Ambrosio, by appointing him military commander and governor.
But quite independently of Zapata, Genovevo de la O's *guerrilleros*
north of Cuernavaca had already ambushed one of Huerta's columns
as it was approaching the city.

Meanwhile, Madero decided — yet again! — to negotiate with
Emiliano Zapata. On August 13, he arrived in Cuernavaca. The next
day he telephoned Zapata, who reiterated that he was ready to retire

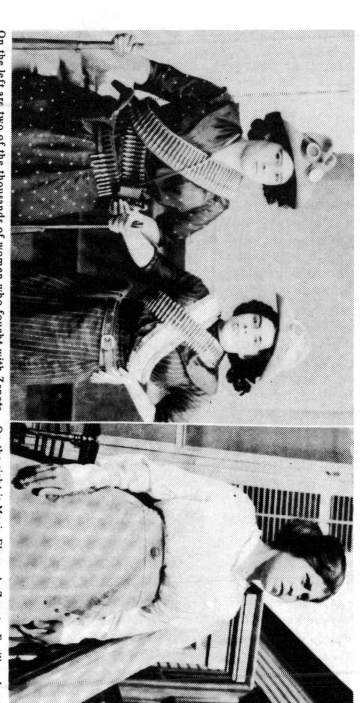

On the left are two of the thousands of women who fought with Zapata. On the right is Maria Flores de Zapata, Emiliano's wife

to his *rancho*, and that the Liberation Army was prepared to demobilise completely except for a small 'select force' to guarantee public
order, if Madero would promise to solve the land question, withdraw
all Federal troops and remove from office unpopular officials and
jefes politicos from the old Diaz regime. When informed, the
interim President, de la Barra, refused to consider such proposals.
He told Madero to assert his authority. Under no circumstances
should he confer with the Morelos rebels. At the same time, General
Huerta was moving in for 'the kill:' he would deal with Zapata
and the Morelos *insurrectos* once and for all.

On August 15, General Jose Gonzalez Salas, the then head of the
War Department, informed Huerta in Cuernavaca that a Federal
column was advancing on Puebla, and would continue towards
Jonacatepec — and that he should inform Madero that if Zapata
did not agree immediately to the complete disarmament of the
Zapatistas — 'that very day' — the Federal Army would commence
operations against them at Yautepec. Thereupon, Huerta moved
his troops towards Yautepec. Zapata, he ordered, must submit
unconditionally.

But Madero decided to confer again with Zapata. He persuaded
his cabinet to agree to suspend all offensive operations against the
Liberation Army for the time being. And he exacted a promise from
General Huerta to cease hostilities 'for at least twenty-four hours.'
But Huerta continued to march on Yautepec. Zapata accused the
government of deliberately fomenting a conflict; he also charged
Madero with 'half-way' measures in not allowing the revolution to
follow its natural course. Huerta, instead of complying with government orders, informed the cabinet that he was 'consolidating his
forces' on the road to Yautepec. Again, he was ordered to maintain
his position.

Reluctantly, he complied and halted his advance; though he sent
some of his troops on ahead to burn down a few huts of local
rancheros. This brought forth protests from a number of village
councils in the area. They telegraphed de la Barra, demanding that
Federal forces be withdrawn from Morelos. De la Barra instructed
his government officials not to answer them. Zapata also telegraphed de la Barra: 'The people want their rights respected. They
want to be paid attention to, and listened to. Just because they

make a protest, nobody can try to shut them up with bayonets.'
Zapata received no reply either.

Francisco Madero and Emiliano Zapata met in Cuautla on the
morning of August 18. Don Francisco gave Emiliano an *abrazo*.
After breakfast at the Hotel San Diego, and a short preliminary
conference with Zapata, Madero addressed a large crowd of
Zapatistas in the Cuautla public gardens and plaza from the balcony
of the Municipal Palace.

Sensing the feelings of the crowd, he said: 'Our enemies do not
rest . . . They would like to make it appear that I have no control
over the chiefs who aided me in the revolution . . . They say that I
am a great patriot, and a sincere man, but that I lack energy . . .
that I lack the abilities to govern because I have not ordered General
Zapata shot . . . Such an act would not require either bravery or
energy. One only needs to be an assassin and a criminal to shoot
one of the most valiant soldiers of the Liberation Army of the South.'

Madero then reaffirmed his faith in the justice of the *Zapatsitas'*
cause, and called for a new revolutionary union against reactionary
intrigues. He knew, he concluded, that the rebels of the South would
always be ready to answer the first call to take up arms to defend
liberty and justice. He was politely applauded.

The ensuing conference got under way during the afternoon, and
proceeded quite amiably. Besides Zapata, all the local Morelos
chiefs and civilian delegates from surrounding *pueblos* took part. It
was agreed that demobilisation would – again! – begin the next
day, that the chiefs would be guaranteed immunity, that Raul
Madero should be commander of the Morelos military zone, that all
Federal troops would be withdrawn from the state and return to
Mexico City forthwith, and be replaced by 'revolutionary' contingents from the states of Hidalgo and Veracruz, that Colonel Eduardo
Hay, a staunch liberal *Maderista*, be appointed governor and the
forthcoming state elections proceed. The land question was not,
however, discussed.

Zapata was not entirely happy about the demobilisation of the
Liberation Army while Federal troops remained; but on the follow-
ing day, the Morelos chiefs began demobilising some of their forces.
The Federals still did not move out. De la Barra was annoyed at
Madero's suggestion that the campaign against the *Zapatistas* was a

reactionary plot; he also contended that Morelos was in rebellion against Madero's own government – which was largely true. He, therefore, ordered Francisco Figueroa to establish 'order' at all costs, and he instructed General Huerta to attack Jonacatepec immediately. As Huerta's forces approached the town, a municipal official came out waving a white flag – and was fired upon. The Federals encircled the town. Madero once again appealed to de la Barra to restrain Huerta. And another truce was arranged. This lasted forty-eight hours. Zapata returned to Villa de Ayala to organise the final discharge of the Liberation Army of the South, which was to begin when he arrived in Cuautla the next morning.

But by August 22, de la Barra had still not appointed Eduardo Hay governor of the state; nor had he begun the evacuation of Federal troops. Indeed, he had reinforced the garrison of Cuerna-vaca with more troops armed with machine-guns. The Morelos chiefs, therefore, refused to lay down their arms. And some of them were almost in open rebellion against General Zapata for accepting Madero's word. Emiliano's brother Eufemio, at the time the worse for drink, said that they should shoot Madero. But Emiliano managed to calm him and most of the chiefs. A very dis-illusioned Francisco Madero finally returned to Mexico City.

Two days later, Federal troops began to encircle Cuautla. Aided by past experience, and a perfect knowledge of the ground, Zapata extricated the major part of his force from the town before Huerta could entrap them. Furious, Huerta ordered immediate pursuit. Zapata split his forces. He and some of his men retreated south to the Hacienda de la Chinameca; while the main body of the *Zapatistas* rode on further south to the easily defended country of Quila Mula. The Federals were, nevertheless, hot on Zapata's heels.

Exhausted, Zapata and about fifty of the 'Death Legion' rested at the *hacienda*. But just before midnight on August 30, Emiliano was awakened by an outburst of gunfire. He could hear shouts and the trampling of feet. A troop of Federals had rode in. Zapata threw open the large casement window, jumped into the garden below and, in the dark, ran through the grounds. He and a number of his men managed to escape through the sugar-cane fields. Fortunately, due to lack of forage near the house, they had been compelled to quarter their horses in a small pasture some distance away. Followed by rather wild gunfire from the Federals, Zapata mounted his horse, Relampago, and sped away into the night. The next day, Huerta arrived at the *hacienda* only to find that his hated — and elusive — enemy had gone. Emiliano Zapata and about twenty of his men were galloping hard towards Quila Mula.

In Mexico City, Madero also had his problems. For some time, he had been arguing that the old Anti-Re-electionist Party had served its purpose and had, in fact, disintegrated; he, therefore, proposed a new party — the Partido Constitucional Progresista — to take its place. Francisco Vazquez Gomez and other *Maderistas* opposed the idea; but Madero went ahead with his plans. The first convention of the new party met in Mexico City on August 27, 1911. There were 1,500 delegates. Madero was acclaimed leader as well as the party's presidential candidate.

Congress agreed that the presidential election be held on October 1. Madero appealed for an orderly election. He was opposed by an old *Porfirista* general, Bernado Reyes, who, after a mob of *Maderistas* had beaten him up, withdrew from the campaign.

The election was merely to elect presidential electors, who would then elect a President on October 15. Reyes' friends — just as in the days of Don Porfirio — charged fraud and manipulation. It was obvious that Francisco Madero would become President and Pino Suarez Vice-President. The election was possibly the most honest that Mexico had ever witnessed — which was not saying a lot. Nor did a very large percentage of the population vote either. Nevertheless, Madero received ninety-eight per cent of the votes cast. But despite his victory at the polls, he had already lost a considerable amount of popular support not only in Morelos and the South but also in many northern parts of the country as well.

SAFE in Quila Mula, Emiliano Zapata became quite taciturn, even morose. He thought deeply about recent events. He often sat alone — silent. Something had happened to him. During the past weeks of endless talks with Madero and others, a 'new man' was being born: out of the broodings of a nature generally cautious, patient, prudent and self-disciplined, had emerged certain definite conclusions — that the revolution was but half won; that a *politico's* promise was worth nothing, and that the old conquistadorial masters of Mexico were as strong as ever. Yet at the same time, Zapata's views and ideas had, since 1909, broadened. In moments of conversation with such people as Gildado Magana, Emilio Vazquez Gomez and Antonio Diaz Soto y Gama he had acquired a new sense of the tasks ahead, a new dimension. He realised that Mexico's rulers were not going to give up their power, privileges and wealth without a long and bitter struggle. And he remarked to his friend, Otilio Montano: 'This revolution is not like other revolutions . . . This is a fight to end, once and for all, what began 400 years ago.'

Emiliano Zapata and the Morelos chiefs prepared themselves for a long fight.

From the beginning of September, Morelos was to be, once again, in open rebellion, not only against General Huerta and the interim President, de la Barra, but also the vacilating 'liberal,' Francisco Madero. Throughout September and October, guerrilla warfare raged in the state. Huerta tried vainly to come to grips with the *Zapatistas*; but rapier-like thrusts by the Liberation Army continually harassed the Federals without allowing them to engage. the *Zapatistas* in open battle. This was guerrilla strategy. A small force of about 400 *Zapatistas* under the command of Proculo Capistran made contact with the Federals, and then retreated steadily southwards, while Zapata took the main column on a long march further south, then eastwards into Puebla, made a feint on Mexico City and, with another forced march, cut across Huerta's rear and destroyed his army. The *Zapatistas'* tactic was: never engage the enemy except from cover, ambush him, flank him, draw him on and, when he is exhausted, attack in force and then fade away. And this is what the *Zapatistas* did.

Many *peones* from the villages and *haciendas* continued to join the Liberation Army. Zapata now had almost 3,000 horsemen. On October 10, they threatened Cuautla, but did not attack it. Instead, they moved north, occupied *pueblos* in the Federal District, and then made an audacious attack on Milpa Alta, less than 25 kilometres from the centre of Mexico City! Meanwhile, Huerta was again moving south, chasing the shadows of a non-existent *Zapatista* army near the state line.

The attack on Milpa Alta – so close to the centre of Mexico City – precipitated an immediate government crisis. The Liberation Army of the South was a force to be reckoned with. A number of ministers resigned. The Minister of War, Venustiano Carranza, telegraphed General Huerta angrily saying that while he – Huerta – had been sent to Morelos to annihilate Zapata, and was presumably disporting himself somewhere on the Puebla or Guerrero borders, Zapata and the Liberation Army were attacking Mexico City. Huerta, baffled and finally drunk, proceeded northwards through Morelos towards the capital, where his troops were continually harassed by guerrilla forces.

Government ministers continued to resign; and at Madero's repeated urgings, General Huerta was replaced. On November 6, Madero was inaugurated President of the Republic. Almost the first thing that he did was to write a letter to his representative in Cuautla.

'Let Zapata know,' he wrote, 'that the only thing I can accept is that he immediately surrender unconditionally, and that all his soldiers immediately lay down their arms. In this case, I will pardon his soldiers for the crime of rebellion, and he will be given a passport so that he can settle outside the state. Inform him that his rebellious attitude is damaging my government greatly, and that I cannot tolerate that it continue under any circumstances.'

Madero appointed General Casso Lopez as the new general in Morelos – with instructions to wipe out the *Zapatistas*. And almost immediately he surrounded Zapata at Villa de Ayala with a small force of Federals. Zapata decided to retreat in order. He and his small escort of horsemen fought off the Federals until nightfall, and then slipped through their lines and escaped. Once again they headed into Puebla and the mountains, recruiting men on the way. Nevertheless, General Lopez, like Huerta before him, made sorry work of pacifying Morelos. In revenge for military humiliation, and convinced that, actively or passively every Morelense was a *Zapatista*, he set about the systematic destruction of many villages and *pueblos* and the hanging and torturing of as many *peones* and *rancheros* as his troops could find. All of which brought more and more recruits to the blood-red banner of *Zapatismo*.

*

CHAPTER VI

PLAN DE AYALA

THROUGHOUT the summer and autumn of 1911, the Mexico City press continually accused Emiliano Zapata and the Liberation Army of being bandits. *El Imparcial* – which was far from being imparcial about anything! – invariably referred to Zapata as that *bandido* or, even more sensationally, as *El Atila del Sur* – the Attila of the South. Harry H. Dunn, the American journalist wrote that Zapata was quite possibly the most powerful outlaw in the known history of the world; and he always called the Liberation Army 'the horde.' Even Mrs. Leone Moates, who had met Zapata, described him as 'a bandit, but an admirable man.'

Emiliano talked about these accusations with a number of friends and with the chiefs, saying that no newspapers tell the people the truth. He remarked that 'the enemies of the country, and of freedom of the people, have always denounced as bandits those who sacrifice themselves for the noble causes of the people.'

It was, therefore, agreed that Zapata and his friend, the former schoolteacher, Otilio Montano, draw up a statement and plan setting out their objectives in an attempt to show that they were not bandits, but were concerned with justice and, above all, the return of their lands, their *ejidos*, to the *peones*. *Zapatismo* was not banditry – and they would prove it! Later, in November, Montano and Zapata went to the little village of Miquetzingo, near Ayoxustla in southeast Puebla; and there for six days they worked on the draft of what was to be the famous *Plan de Ayala*.

In a way, the *Plan de Ayala* had been evolving for more than fifty years – ever since the government of Diaz and the *hacendados* had begun to steal the people's lands. But the *Plan de Ayala* was, to some extent, a composite document, as well as a compromise. The ideas were Zapata's and Montano's, as well as those of various chiefs. Both Zapata and Montano had also been influenced by Ricardo Flores Magon and other radicals.* Nevertheless, though the completed

*Some writers have argued that the PLAN DE AYALA is directly based upon Magon's MANIFESTO of September 23rd, 1911. It is this writer's view that this is not likely (though some of the phrases are similar), as copies of the MANIFESTO do not appear to have reached Morelos until late January or early February, 1912.

draft was largely written by the former schoolteacher, the *Plan de Ayala* was as simple and direct as Zapata. And there were no empty promises. It was not a *politico's* manifesto.

When it was finished, Zapata called a junta of chiefs to assemble at the neighbouring mountain town of Ayoxustla to discuss and, he hoped, sign the *Plan de Ayala*. By November 27, many of the chiefs, together with a large number of *Zapatistas*, camped in the Sierra de Ayoxustla. The *Plan* was discussed. The next day, they arranged themselves in a vast half-moon by contingents, each chief at the head of his column, in front of a little abandoned shepherd's hut. A small table was placed before the door. Montano deposited his writing kit on the table. A Mexican flag was brought out, and was flown from a makeshift pole. Someone set off a few fireworks.

At eleven o'clock Emiliano Zapata quietly and rather hesitatingly began to speak.

'*Amigos*, the time has come for us to make plain to ourselves and all Mexico why we are fighting, and what we fight for. And so, with Montano here, I have been trying for the past few days to set down in words why we took up arms, and what we demand before we lay them down . . . I want you to listen very carefully . . . Then I shall ask you, chief by chief, to set your hands to what is written . . . Any man who does not wish to sign is free to depart without illfeeling on our part . . . '

Zapata then asked Montano to read what they had written. Montano stood on the table, and began to read aloud.

'Liberating plan of the sons of the state of Morelos . . . .

We who undersigned, constituted in a revolutionary junta to sustain and carry out the promises which the revolution of November 20, 1910, just past, made to our country, declare solemnly before the face of the civilised world which judges us, and before the nation to which we belong, and to which we call, propositions which we have formulated to end the tyranny which oppresses us and redeem the fatherland from the dictatorships which are imposed on us, which propositions are determined in the following plan.

Taking into consideration that the Mexican people led by Don Francisco Madero went to shed their blood to reconquer liberties and recover rights which had been trampled on, and not for a man to take possession of power, violating the sacred principles which he took an oath to defend under the slogan "Effective Suffrage and No Re-election", outraging thus the faith, the cause of justice,

64

and the liberties of the people; taking into consideration that that man to whom we refer is Don Francisco Madero, the same who initiated the above-cited revolution, who imposed his will and influence on the provisional government of the ex-President of the Republic, Attorney Francisco L. de la Barra, causing with this deed repeated sheddings of blood and multiplicate misfortunes in a manner deceitful and ridiculous, having no intentions other than satisfying his personal ambitions, his boundless instincts as a tyrant, and his profound disrespect for the fulfilment of the pre-existing laws written with the revolutionary blood of Ayutla.

Taking into account that the so-called chief of the liberating revolution of Mexico, Don Francisco Madero, through lack of integrity and the highest weakness, did not carry to a happy end the revolution which gloriously he initiated with the help of the people, since he left standing most of the governing powers and corrupted elements of oppression of the dictatorial government of Porfirio Diaz . . . . '

Montano paused, and then continued.

'Taking into consideration that the so-often repeated Francisco Madero has tried with the brute force of bayonets to shut up and drown in blood the *pueblos* who ask, solicit, or demand from him the fulfilment of the promises of the revolution, calling them bandits and rebels, condemning them to a war of extermination without conceding or granting a single one of the guarantees which reason, justice, and the law prescribe; taking equally into consideration that the President of the Republic, Francisco Madero, had made effective suffrage a bloody trick on the people, already against the will of the people imposing Attorney Jose M. Pino Suarez in the Vice-presidency of the Republic, or imposing governors of the states men designated by him, like the so-called general, Ambrosio Figueroa, scourge and tyrant of the people of Morelos, or entering into scandalous co-operation with the *cientifico* party, feudal landlords, and oppressive bosses, enemies of the revolution proclaimed by him, so far as to forge new chains and follow the pattern of a new dictatorship more shameful and more terrible than that of Porfirio Diaz, for it has been clear and patent that he has outraged the sovereignty of the states, trampling on the law without respect for lives or interests, as happened in the state of Morelos.

For these considerations we declare the aforementioned Madero inept at realising the promises of the revolution of which he was the author, because he betrayed the principles with which he tricked the will of the people, and was able to get into power; incapable of governing, because he has no respect for the law and the justice of the *pueblos*, and a traitor to the fatherland, because he is humiliating in blood and fire Mexicans who want liberties, so as to please the *cientificos*, landlords and bosses who enslave us, and from today we begin to continue the revolution begun by him, until we achieve the overthrow of the dictatorial power that exists. Recognition is withdrawn from senor Francisco Madero as chief of the revolution and as President of the Republic, for the reasons which were before expressed, it being attempted to overthrow this official . . . . '

There were murmurs of approval. Montano again continued reading.

'The revolutionary junta of the State of Morelos will admit no transaction or compromises until it achieves the overthrow of the dictatorial elements of Porfirio Diaz and Francisco Madero, for the nation is tired of false men and traitors who make promises like liberators and who, on achieving power, forget them and constitute themselves as tyrants.

As an additional part of our plan we invoke, we give notice: that regarding the fields, timber and water which the landlords, *cientificos,* or *hacendados* have usurped, the *pueblos* or citizens who have titles corresponding to those properties will immediately enter possession of that which they have been despoiled by the bad faith of our oppressors, maintaining at any cost with arms in hand the mentioned possession; and the usurpers who consider themselves with a right to those properties will deduce it before the special tribunals which will be established on the triumph of the revolution.

In virtue of the fact that the immense majority of Mexican *pueblos* and citizens are owners of no more than the land they walk on, suffering the horrors of poverty without being able to improve their social condition in any way, or dedicate themselves to industry or agriculture, because the lands, timber and water are monopolised in a few hands, for this cause there will be expropriated the third part of those monopolies from the powerful proprietors of them, with prior indemnification, in order that the *pueblos* and citizens of Mexico may obtain *ejidos*, colonies and foundations for *pueblos*, or fields for sowing or labouring; and the Mexicans' lack of prosperity and wellbeing may improve in all, and for all.

Regarding the landlords, *hacendados*, and *cientificos* who oppose the present plan directly or indirectly, their goods will be socialised and the two-third parts which otherwise would belong to them will go for indemnification of war, pensions for widows and orphans or the victims who succumb in the struggle for the present plan.

The insurgent military chiefs of the republic who rose up with arms in hand at the voice of Don Francisco Madero, and who oppose with armed force the plan, will be judged traitors to the cause which they defended, since at present many of them, to humour the tyrants, for a fistful of coins, or for bribes or connivance, are shedding the blood of their brothers who claim fulfilment of the promises which Don Francisco made to the nation . . . '

Montano paused.

'Once triumphant, the revolution which we carry into reality, a junta of the principle revolutionary chiefs from the different states will name or designate an interim president of the republic, who will convoke elections for the organisation of the Federal powers.

The principle revolutionary chiefs of eash state will designate in junta the governor of the state to which they belong, and this appointed official will convoke elections for the organisation of the public powers, the object being to avoid compulsory appointments which work to the misfortune of the *pueblos*, like the well-known appointment of Ambrosio Figueroa in the state of Morelos, and others who drive us to the precipice of bloody conflicts, sustained by caprice of the dictator, Madero, and the circle of *cientificos* and *hacendados* who have influenced him.

If President Madero and other dictatorial elements of the present and former regime want to avoid the immense misfortunes which afflict the country, and if they possess true sentiments of love for it, let them make immediate renunciation of the posts they occupy and with that they will with something staunch the grave wounds which they have opened in the bosom of the fatherland, since, if they do not do so, on their heads will fall the blood and the anathema of our brothers.

Mexicans! Consider that the cunning and bad faith of one man is shedding blood in a scandalous manner, because he is incapable of governing; consider that his system of government is choking the fatherland, and trampling with brute force of bayonets on our institutions; and, thus, as we raised up our weapons to elevate him to power, we again raise them up against him for defaulting on his promises to the Mexican people, and for having betrayed the revolution initiated by him. We are not personalists; we are partisans of principles and not of men.

67

Mexican people: support this plan with arms in hand, and you will make the prosperity and well-being of the fatherland. Liberty! Justice! Law!'

As the shouts of acclamation died down, Montano jumped from the table, and Zapata climbed upon it. He spoke briefly.

'*Amigos*! Seek justice from tyrannical governments, including this one we have now, not with your hat in your hand, but with a rifle in your fists . . . . Men of the South, it is better to die on your feet than live on your knees . . . for we tend our arms to everyone except the enemies of the popular cause . . . The land free, free for all, without overseers and without masters, that is the cry of the revolution . . . You have heard the plan. It is for you to decide . . . I want to die a slave to principles, not to men!'

There were cries of '*Viva Zapata!*' and '*Viva la revolucion!*', followed by '*Viva El Plan de Ayala!*'

Then, in single file the chiefs came forward to sign. Some inscribed a labourious signature; some could only make a mark, while Otilio Montano signed for them. But each chief, after he signed, wheeled on his men for a show of hands. And contingent by contingent, they signaled assent. So, to a man the *Plan de Ayala* was approved. Altogether, thirty-eight chiefs signed. They included Proculo Capistran, Francisco Mendoza, Jesus Morales, Jose Trinidad Ruiz and, of course, Otilio Montano and Emiliano and Eufemio Zapata.

Following the junta at Ayoxustla, Zapata moved the Liberation Army, now around 8,000 strong, back into the Morelos mountains near Huautla. And there an old village priest who owned a typewriter agreed to type out several copies of the *Plan de Ayala*. Emiliano kept the original, while the copies were sent by messenger to Mexico City and given to journalists. One copy was shown to Madero, who said that he had no objection to its publication — it would demonstrate to everyone just how crazy Zapata and the Morelos chiefs were. The *Plan* was then published.

DURING December, on the insistence of his brother, Gustavo, Francisco Madero sent another deputation to Zapata. Again, Emiliano was offered a safe passage to another state and a *hacienda*. And again, he refused.

'Madero,' he told the deputation, 'has betrayed me as well as the army and the people of Morelos . . . Most of his original supporters are in jail or persecuted . . . Nobody trusts him any longer, because he has violated all his promises. He is the most fickle, vacillating man I've ever known.'

'What message should we give President Madero?'

'Tell him from me,' replied Zapata, 'to take off for Havana, because if not he can count the days as they go by, and in a month I'll be in Mexico City with 20,000 men, and have the pleasure of going up to Chapultepec Castle and dragging him out of there, and hanging him from one of the highest trees in the park.'

The deputation hastily departed. Emiliano Zapata and the Liberation Army of the South were irrevocably at war with President Francisco Madero.

In fairness to Madero, however, it should be said that he never really understood the land question; he was of the upper class, and did not understand the common people. He believed in things like freedom of the press and elections. He knew there was something wrong. He had seen some of the poverty, hunger and degradation. But he came from the north of the country, and he did not realise that, at least in the south and centre, in the main, the *peones* had never really developed the concept of private land ownership. That the people should imagine that the *ejido* should belong communally to all those who worked upon it was completely alien to his way of thinking. Neither Madero nor his political advisors had given much thought to the *ejidos* or their future. Nor did Madero realise just how much land had been taken from the *peones* and *campesinos* by the *hacendados* and the Mexican state, particularly under President Diaz.

To the extent that Madero was forced to consider the land question, he believed in encouraging the development of smallholdings and *ranchos*; he wanted to see the emergence of a class of prosperous peasant proprietors similar to those he had encountered in France. He was, therefore, mainly concerned with the fate of the largely *mestizo*-owned *ranchos* rather than with the masses of landless Indians. And so, during the summer of 1911, when the *peones* of Morelos, Oaxaca, Puebla and a number of other southern states were taking back some of the land which had previously been sequested from them by the *hacendados*, Madero merely asked the landowners to voluntarily alleviate the people's suffering!

Nevertheless, during December 1911, and January 1912, Madero's government did attempt to tackle the land question in a half-hearted sort of way. A bill was introduced into Congress for the construction

69

of dams and irrigation systems, the reclamation of waste lands, and the purchase of some arable land for resale in small plots. And in February, the government's National Agrarian Commission published a preliminary report, which included the partition of some particularly large estates. The question of *ejidal* holdings had been discussed by the Commission, but no proposals had been made. Most of the members of the Commission, however, favoured the partitioning of the remaining *ejidos* among the *peones* with the proviso that the lands thus granted would be inalienable for twenty years. No one thought that the *peones* should get all their common lands back.

Madero and the government discussed the question of partitioning *ejidos* at some length; and on February 17, they sent a circular letter to all state governors recommending the delimitation of exisiting *ejidal* holdings. A week later, the government ordered a survey of national lands with a view to their possible sale. Some *hacendados* were willing to sell part of their land, but they demanded such a high price that the government could not purchase the land for resale. It was obvious that the plan was going to be a failure. Furthermore, it also caused a government crisis. About sixty 'leftist' *Maderista* congressmen introduced a bill calling for the restoration of the *ejidos* on a communal basis. Naturally, there were strong objections from conservative *Maderista* congressmen. By the beginning of 1913, all Madero's half-hearted attempts at dealing with the agrarian problem had come to nothing. Moreover, much of the old *Porfirista* state machine and bureaucracy, as well as the Federal Army, remained intact.

CHAPTER VII

THE SOUTH AFLAME

IT WAS not only the 'Men from Morelos' with whom Madero had to contend. Mexico was in a continual state of turmoil; and Don Francisco had many enemies – and was making more daily.

On the very day that he took office there was a rebellion against his state governor in Oaxaca. This was quickly suppressed. In Sinaloa, yet another rebellion broke out in December, but this too was defeated. Two days after Madero's inauguration, a plot by some Federal generals to overthrow his government by a violent coup was discovered. And then, at last, General Bernado Reyes attempted what Madero had said he was intending to do during the summer: he rebelled.

BURNING HACIENDAS

Reyes began to organise an uprising from San Antonio in the United States. On December 13, he crossed the Texas border with 600 followers, expecting a nationwide response; but except for a few very minor *Reyista* uprisings scattered around the country, the nation was not interested in General Reyes. 'I called upon the army, and I called upon the people,' he said. 'but the days passed, and not a single individual came to join me.' On Christmas Day he surrendered.

But that was not the end of Madero's troubles . . .

There were yet to be more rebellions – and one coup d'etat.

A far more dangerous movement against Madero began to gain momentum during December. Its leader was Pascual Orozco, one of the ablest of the *Maderista* commanders. Orozco felt that he had been treated badly by Madero. He wanted to be a state governor, but had been defeated in the election; he had wanted to execute the Federal commander at Ciudad Juarez, but he had been stopped by Madero, and he had demanded 50,000 pesos for his services to the 'revolution,' but had received only 5,000. Pascual Orozco was, to say the least, a frustrated man. On March 3, 1912, he openly rebelled against Madero. A number of *hacendados* gave him encouragement and, more important, plenty of money and arms.

In Mexico City, General Jose Salas, the Minister of War and a relative of Don Francisco, resigned his post to take command of the Federal Army. But during the ensuing conflict with *Orozquista* forces on the arid plains of southern Chihuahua, Salas was wounded and, after being ordered to retreat by Madero, committed suicide. A wave of hysteria gripped Mexico City. The government panicked, and the cabinet insisted – against Madero's advice – on recalling General Victoriano Huerta to stop the *Orozquistas*. The old *Porfirista* general, Huerta, had been waiting for such a call.

Huerta reassembled and reorganised the Federal Army. Then he went north to direct the campaign in person. But Huerta seemed to move very slowly; he also came into conflict with 'Pancho' Villa. Nevertheless, despite apparent slowness, Huerta went from victory to victory. By September, Orozco was defeated. He fled to the United States. And his supporters melted away.

But even before the last *Orozquista* rebels had been quelled, Felix Diaz, Don Porfirio's nephew, began a rebellion in Veracruz. Don Felix was plump and vain, and he had a reputation for being a womaniser. He was also over-confident. The Federal Army, aided by units of the Federal Navy, soon quashed his attempts to overthrow

Madero.

Moreover, under his regime, business was booming. Imports remained steady and exports showed an increase. But the conditions of the poor did not improve. Almost ten million *peones* starved, or at best, suffered from malnutrition.

AND throughout 1912, Morelos remained in arms. Indeed, the *Zapatista* struggle went on and on and, sometimes, right into the southern suburbs of Mexico City itself. The government's efforts to destroy *Zapatismo* were unavailing, even though a succession of Federal generals were able to contain the Liberation Army with at least some degree of effectiveness.

The *Zapatistas* did not have either a highly structured army or a political organisation. The Liberation Army of the South was, of necessity, a people in arms — the twentieth century's first people in arms, in fact. The junta which issued the *Plan de Ayala* merely comprised most of the Morelos chiefs. Nor, at that time, did the Liberation Army have any full-time officials or secretaries; and Zapata's chief-of-staff, Abraham Martinez, was still in Puebla City jail. Furthermore, two important chiefs — Felipe Neri and Genovevo de la O — did not adhere to the Ayala junta. Nevertheless, their aims were the same as Zapata's.

The Liberation Army of the South was unlike the other armies of the Mexican Revolution. It lacked money and financial support. There was always — or nearly always — a chronic shortage of military equipment, including both artillery and machine-guns. Ammunition was generally scarce.

The *Zapatistas* adopted the tactics of guerrilla warfare, at which they became extremely adept. Following the struggles of 1911, *Zapatista* strategy shifted against the capture of, and often subsequent withdrawal from, small towns. Large pitched battles were avoided.

The liberation Army had, by the beginning of January 1912, grown to around 12,000 men. It organised itself into small, largely self-supporting bands, based upon the villages which, in turn, could be marshalled rapidly into much larger contingents where and when necessary. Such bands varied in size from a score to, perhaps, a couple of hundred. Each band from different parts of Morelos and, at various periods, other southern states, would have its own elected chief who, again, in varying degrees, owed his allegiance to General Zapata, the Supreme Chief of the Liberation Army of the South. Nevertheless, the Liberation Army was largely decentralised. The local village communities supplied the men — and sometimes the women —of the army with whatever food and sustenance they could. And, where possible, the Liberation Army established the procedure of alternating the *soldados* between three-month periods of 'active service' and working in the fields.

'Before such tactics,' says Pinchon, 'the Federal columns — launched again and again with bands playing, flags flying — again and again came limping home, starving, decimated, terrified, mutinous.'

In the north of Morelos, the very independent *Zapatista* chief, Genovevo de la O, from the *pueblo* of Santa Maria near Cuernavaca, became the terror of the Ajuscos. Basing himself on the precipitous wooded cone of the Cerro itself, dominating the Cima Divide — the only western railroad pass between Cuernavaca and Mexico City — he set himself the task of 'cutting the military throat' of Morelos. He boasted that he and his men would blow up every troop-train coming into the state.

By February, 1912, there were 1,000 Federals and more than 5,000 *rurales* in Morelos. But they could only effectively hold the towns. They had almost no control over the countryside. Moreover, their lines of communication were continually being cut. This was particularly so with regard to the railroads; for Genovevo de la O was true to his word. Very few trains got through. Harry H. Dunn describes one such raid, on this occasion by Zapata himself.

'A government troop-train, made of steel gondolas and armoured box-cars, carrying 1,500 men, was sent over the Interoceanic Railway to Venta de Cruz, a junction at which a spur track to Pachuca leaves the main line from Mexico City. The War Office of the Madero government announced this as an "expedition which would disperse and destroy the *Zapatista* rabble." Emiliano's engineers, who had not heard about the dispersal or destruction, planted dynamite in a suitable place beneath the rails . . . .

As the troop-train rolled along one of the hidden *Zapatistas* pressed the plunger on a simple contact box. Rails and ties lifted ahead and beneath the locomotive. A section of the rails, with ties attached, folded backward over part of the engine so that the smoke-stack and steam-dome projected through the trellis of the track. The tender was wrecked. The engineer and fireman, only slightly bruised, could not move their engine backward or forward . . . .

The soldiers stayed in their armoured cars. The countryside was quiet, save for the curses of the engineer and fireman, until an unarmed man, riding a mule and carrying a white flag, came out of the brush.

He bore a message from Emiliano Zapata to the commander of the troops, a colonel of abundant uniform and considerable sword. General Zapata proposed that if the *Maderista* forces would remain in the cars, doing no fighting, he would provide them with an engine, hooked on to the rear of the train, which would tow them, unharmed, back to Mexico City. As this proposition was made the man on the mule dipped his white flag. Instantly, armed men arose on all sides of the trapped train. Machine-guns fully assembled, were trundled forward out fo the *bosque*.

The colonel delivered an oration on the subject himself, but agreed to the terms. Thereupon a switch engine, picked up at the junction, backed into view and took on the troop-train. which was unhooked from the trapped engine. The engineer and fireman were transferred from their cab to that of the new locomotive, and all rolled back down the line towards the national capital. The arrival of this expeditionary force in Mexico City, defeated without a shot, and alive only because of the clemency of Zapata, was a greater blow to the Madero government than the destruction of the troops and train would have been.'

NOT only Morelos, but also Guerrero, Mexico State, Michoacan, Puebla and even Oaxaca were all aflame. On January 17, Madero accepted Figueroa's resignation from the governorship of Morelos. And two days later, martial law was declared in Guerrero, Morelos, Puebla, Tlaxacala and thirteen districts of Mexico State.

At the end of the month, over 3,000 *Zapatistas*, under the combined command of Salazar, Vazquez and de la O, gathered around the state capital of Cuernavaca, from Tepoztlan to Temixco to Huitzilac. Their base was de la O's village of Santa Maria, on the edge of the old volcano just a few kilometres from Cuernavaca. By January 26, the Federals attempted to take Santa Maria, but after forty-eight hours' fighting were unable to shift the *Zapatistas*. The struggle then moved back to Cuernavaca, where Genovevo de la O's *guerrilleros* attacked the city almost continually for over a week. But the Federals held out. And after a short lull, the Federal commander made a desperate move against the *Zapatistas* — he again sent a force against Santa Maria. And this time he was successful. His troops set light not only to the *pueblo* but also the surrounding woods, and the *Zapatista* base. The Federals soaked all the village buildings with kerosene, fired them, and then retreated. Artillery shells, exploding in the woods, set them alight. By evening, the village was in ashes, and most of the woods, including the *Zapatista* base, were charred timber. De la O's daughter was trapped in one house which was set on fire. She did not escape the flames. Nor did any other villagers.

The *Zapatista* attacks against Cuernavaca and a number of Morelos towns continued, under various chiefs, for over a month before petering out. Zapata had not been in agreement with such tactics, as they had been unsuccessful in the past, but he did not appear to oppose the other chiefs, or he had, possibly, been over-ruled. However, the government of Madero had already begun a campaign of terror against the entire population of Morelos. Villages were systematically set alight, and their inhabitants – if found alive – were 'resettled' in concentration camps elsewhere in Mexico. Hostages were taken.

The government and the Federal Army were convinced that the whole population of Morelos, excluding the *hacendados*, a few hangers-on and a number of rich merchants, supported the *Zapatistas* or were *Zapatistas* at least in spirit. And they were right! In the words of an old *Zapatista* twenty years after: 'In those days, even the stones were *Zapatistas.*' *Zapatismo*, therefore, had to be destroyed, even if this meant ruining the state and either killing or dispersing all the people in the attempt.

Following Figueroa's resignation, the government appointed Brigadier-General Juvencio Robles, a veteran of the Indian wars and an 'expert' in extermination, as the new military commander in Morelos and southern Mexico. Within days of his arrival in the state, he had Zapata's mother-in-law, sister-in-law and Emiliano's own sister, Luz, arrested, and taken to Cuernavaca as hostages. He then put his 'resettlement' policy into operation. On February 15, Federal troops swooped on the little village of Nexpa, along the Chinameca River, near the Guerrero state line. They found one hundred-and-thirty-six people there, of whom most were women and children. They were all rounded up and taken, under guard, to Jojutla where they were kept under police surveillance. That was only the beginning, however. Many other villages, including Zapata's own village of San Miguel Anencuilco, were also destroyed. Some *ranchos* were also reduced to rubble. Many *peones* throughout Morelos were driven from their homes, while others were executed by firing squads or by the old custom of *ley fuga.*

Nevertheless, some of the local *hacendados* and planters were getting worried. Not only were the *Zapatistas* waging war on them, but the Federal forces were not particularly careful whom they attacked, or where they went. The planters, moreover, had to think of the sugar-cane harvest.

By April, the *Zapatistas* were, yet again, on the offenisve. But their ammunition soon ran out. There was something of a stalemate; and in May, a number of *Zapatista* chiefs were forced to suspend operations. Genovevo de la O's *guerrilleros* moved up into Mexico State and, on one occasion, as far as Hidalgo. And after an indecisive junta, at which both Neri and Salazar announced their withdrawal from active participation, Zapata also decided to withdraw the main force of *Zapatistas* into eastern Guerrero. *Zapatista* bands made two or three forays into the suburbs of Mexico City. But that was all.

EARLY in May, 1912, Madero recalled General Robles, and sent him to Puebla. There were also dissensions within the *Zapatista* ranks – and in Morelos, during June and July the rains were very heavy indeed. Furthermore, a number of *Zapatista* spokesmen, including Gildaro Magana and Luis Mendoza, had been arrested while visiting Mexico City. One of the Flores Magon brothers, Jesus, who had gone over to the Madero government, and had been appointed Minister of the Interior, felt that Zapata might be prepared to come to terms, or even surrender. So he sent a secret envoy to Zapata's headquarters; but Zapata told the envoy that he would not give in, or come to terms with 'the traitor' Madero.

Meanwhile, Zpaata began to quietly gather supplies. Genovevo de la O and his men returned to Morelos – and immediately began to attack Federal troop and supply trains.

General Felipe Angeles replaced Robles as commander of the Federal forces in Morelos and the south. Angeles was a military intellectual and a 'liberal.' He did not burn *pueblos*. He brought yet another olive branch. Government policy changed. The government now supported the more respectable reformist 'revolutionaries' in Morelos. And they, in turn, proposed laws in favour of small rural and urban proprietors and landowners, while, at the same time, recommending a ten per cent tax increase on the large *hacendados*.

Many *Zapatistas* quietly returned to their *pueblos* and *ranchos . . .*

Angeles was very pleased with himself. Throughout September and much of October, there were no military operations or *Zapatista* raids in Morelos. Most of the chiefs, including General

77

Zapata, were prepared to wait and see what happened.

But the Morelos state legislature kept postponing the various reform measures. Other reformist bills were also voted down. The legislature was obviously not going to act against the *hacendados* and planters, or demand the return of stolen lands. Parliamentary methods, both national and local, appeared more than useless in the struggle for land and justice. The *Zapatistas* soon realised this. By the end of October, they were on the move again.

On November 1, Zapata and many of the Morelos chiefs held a junta, at which they agreed to levy a weekly 'tax' on a number of *haciendas* in both Morelos and Puebla. If the planter did not agree to pay, his cane fields would go up in flames. Some planters paid; others refused. Their fields were set alight. Although Federal troops remained in the state capital, Cuernavaca, the Liberation Army of the South was now in a much stronger position than it had been earlier in the year. By mid-winter, it had a minimum of 20,000 well-armed and mounted men scattered throughout five or six southern states of Mexico.

Dunn comments:

'Thus as 1912 became 1913, the 20,000 or more *Zapatistas*, well-mounted, abundantly munitioned, fed by the secondary army organised by Juana Mola Mendez, lay in the form of a giant U to the south, east and west of Mexico City. They formed probably the most mobile force of its size ever assembled in the Western Hemisphere. To this mobility they owed their continued existence. Emiliano Zapata understood quite well that sudden, hard, merciless attack is the best defence.'

Such was the Liberation Army – the fighting arm of *Zapatismo*.

CHAPTER VIII

HUERTA

THE recall of General Victoriano Huerta, in March 1912, was tantamount to Madero signing his own death sentence.

Throughout the summer both men were at odds with Huerta demanding – and usually getting – autonomy of action against 'rebels.' General Huerta was a Diaz man. As early as October, 1911, the United States government had been informed by one of its agents that Huerta was involved in plans for a *coup d'etat* against Madero.

Venustiano Carranza

Felix Diaz

Victoriano Huerta

Porfirio Diaz.

Following his successful campaign against Orozco he had been put on the inactive list, ostensibly because he had an eye infection; but the most likely reason was that he had incurred a 1,500,000 pesos expense account, much of which ultimately found its way into real estate.

Huerta was a military man through and through — and Madero was always suspicious of military men. Madero, however, true to his 'liberal' ideals, never attempted to destroy the power of the old Federal Army. In the end, the Federal Army was to destroy him.

Unlike most Mexican military leaders, Huerta was a full-blooded Indian — a descendant of the Aztecs — who, as a boy, had taught himself to read and write. Later, he attended the Chapultepec Military Academy. He was brave and, by Mexican standards, was considered a military genius. He was a disciplinarian with his troops; but he had the army behind him. He was the most formidable foe Zapata had encountered. But by 1912, he was bald and suffered from bad eyesight. Of him Mrs. Leone B. Moats comments: 'A tough old brave, in his sixties, carelessly clad in the dress of the conquering white . . . Huerta had every pleasurable vice known to men: women, liquor, and war meant life to him.' He was indeed a heavy drinker of cognac; and it was said that his only friends were two Europeans — Messrs. Hennessey and Martell! Huerta also wanted power.

His opportunity came in February 1913. On February 4, a young army officer gave Madero's brother, Gustavo, a list of people who, he claimed, were involved in a plot to overthrow the government. Included in the list were Felix Diaz and Bernado Reyes, General Manuel Mondragon, a former *Porfirista* chief who had recently returned from exile in Cuba, and a number of other generals — including General Victoriano Huerta. Gustavo rushed to tell Don Francisco, but he would not believe him. There had been so many plots against him during the last twelve months. Anyway, he considered most of those named to be basically loyal.

But the plot was real.

The *coup* was scheduled for March 16, but as Gustavo Madero had postponed a visit to Japan, and was beginning to organise a counter-*coup*, the plotters brought the date forward. Rumours of the plot spread throughout Mexico City; but Madero still did nothing.

Just after 2 a.m. on Sunday, February 9, a column of soldiers moved along Chapultepec Avenue towards the centre of the city. At the same time, six hundred cadets from the Tlalpan Military School headed for the National Palace. The first group marched on the old prison of Santiago Tlaltelolco, where they released Bernado Reyes and the other prisoners, who set the building on fire; the other column, led by Mondragon, marched to the penitentiary where they released Felix Diaz. The plotters had about 3,000 men armed with six cannons and fourteen machine-guns. The column led by Diaz and Mondragon halted just before reaching the Zocalo, whilst the other column, led by Ruiz and Reyes, advanced directly on the National Palace. But Gustavo Madero had gained control of the Palace with loyal troops. Reyes led the attack on the Palace – and was riddled with machine-gun fire. The shooting lasted about ten minutes; then the attackers retreated.

Meanwhile, Francisco Madero, at Chapultepec Castle, decided to ride to the National Palace. There was some sporadic firing in the streets. Madero was persuaded to take cover in the Daguerre photographical studios, where Huerta – quite by coincidence of course! – joined him. Madero thereupon appointed Huerta commander of the *Plaza*. On his arrival at the Palace, Huerta immediately executed his old military colleague, Gregorio Ruiz, for no apparent reason. And so Madero established himself, together with his brother and Huerta, in the National Palace. Francisco appointed – in his absence – General Angeles chief-of-staff of the Ministry of War; and he put Huerta in charge of 6,000 'loyal' troops. He telegraphed Angeles to break off all engagements with Zapata and the Liberation Army and to return, with 1,000 Federal troops, to Mexico City forthwith.

On February 11, the anti-*Maderistas* began firing their cannons towards the National Palace. Huerta replied from the Palace. But except for one stray shell neither side scored a hit. Machine-gunners, again from both sides, sprayed the streets with their fire; and at the end of the day, over 500 people had been killed – all of them civilians not involved in the conflict. In fact, both sides hit almost everything in sight except their supposed targets. The so-called battle lasted ten days, and has gone down in Mexican history as the *Decena Tragica* – the Tragic Ten.

At the end of the ten-day period, over 5,000 people – again, almost all of them civilians – had been killed in Mexico City. Corpses lay in the blazing sun for days on end. Garbage was piled everywhere. All city services ceased. The stink was appalling. But at the same time, 'negotiations' were going on between General Huerta and the rebels.

Huerta met Felix Diaz. Gustavo reported it to his brother. Madero did nothing. Yet Felix Diaz kept calling upon Madero to resign.

On Monday, February 17, Madero's brother took matters into his own hands. A friend of his got Huerta drunk (an easy task) at the National Palace; then Gustavo stepped into the room and disarmed Huerta, and put him under arrest. Later, he brought him before Francisco, and accused him of disloyalty and of parleying with Felix Diaz. Huerta insisted that he was loyal to Madero. Had he not defeated Orozco? Madero was yet again taken in. And Huerta was released.

Next morning, Huerta persuaded Gustavo Madero to have lunch with him in the Gambrinus Restaurant, and talk things over. Surprisingly, Gustavo agreed. Huerta was in a jovial mood and, after drinking awhile, he asked Gustavo to excuse him for a moment as he wanted to make a telephone call. Immediately he had left the room, a group of Federal soldiers rushed in and took Gustavo prisoner, locking him in the gentlemen's lavatory. At the same time — 1.30.p.m. to be precise — more troops entered the National Palace without resistance, where Francisco Madero was holding a cabinet meeting and, after some heated arguments, two Federal officers arrested Madero. One of Madero's ministers drew his revolver. The soldiers then shot and killed Madero's cousin, Marcos Hernandez, who was in the room at the time. Madero was confronted by General Blanquet, a *Porfirista* plotter, who said to him: 'You are my prisoner'. Madero replied: 'I am the President; you are a traitor'. Nevertheless Madero and all his government ministers were overpowered. They were surrounded by disloyal troops.

Huerta informed all foreign embassies that the army had overthrown the government. He appointed himself Provisional President. A new cabinet was named. And in the next election, Felix Diaz would be the only presidential candidate and, as in the days of his uncle, Don Porfirio, would be 'elected' President.

Congress, almost to a man, accepted the situation. The Federal Army and its *Porfirista* allies had ousted Madero with very little effort.

Meanwhile, Gustavo Madero was taken from the restaurant to the Ciudadela, where a mob of about two hundred of Huerta's troops lynched him. He was hacked, bayoneted and shot to pieces. Later, in the evening of February 22, Madero and Suarez, one of Madero's former ministers, were taken from the National Palace in two cars. Both were heavily guarded. Shortly after, a number of shots were heard. Madero and Suarez were found dead, riddled with bullets. The officer in charge of the escort claimed that his convoy had been attacked by a group of men, whom they had, of course, not seen. He and his troop escaped, but, he said, Madero and Suarez had been killed in the crossfire. No one bothered to find out the truth. Huerta's complicity in the murders was assumed, though never proved. He was the Provisional President anyway; and Madero – who a mere two years previously had been hailed as a Mexican Christ – was dead and gone, and that, as they said, was that.

General Victoriano Huerta was now in the presidential saddle, but he too soon found that he was unable to ride the horse . . . . .

DURING the *Decena Tragica* most of the *Zapatista* chiefs continued or resumed their campaign. This was made easier because of Angeles' withdrawal of between 1,000 and 2,000 Federal troops. The Liberation Army of the South occupied a number of towns and *haciendas*. Following Huerta's assumption of power, however, there was some confusion within the *Zapatista* ranks.

Emiliano Zapata and Genovevo de la O knew full well what Huerta was like. They were not fooled. In a letter to a certain Dr. Francisco Vazquez Gomez, Zapata wrote: 'I recommend to you that you please express to your brother, the lawyer Emilio Vazquez Gomez, that my soldiers and I long for peace, but we wish that this peace be in accord with the principles which we sustain and that, if it is not in this form, we will continue fighting for our demands until we conquer or succumb; that if he is determined to enter into agreement with the present government, that in his conscience he will find the result of his work, but I will not depart the slightest from the precepts of the *Plan de Ayala*.'

Nevertheless, there were a number of defections from the *Zapatista* ranks. Otilio Montano welcomed the overthrow of Madero and the Huerta *coup*, but soon changed his mind. Jesus 'One Eye' Morales went to Mexico City, and announced that Zapata and all the chiefs would soon lay down their arms; and some of the chiefs including Simon Beltran, Joaquin Mirander and the independent chief, Jose Trinidad Ruiz, did in fact come to terms with Huerta – for the time being.

Between them, the *Zapatistas* now controlled almost all of Morelos. So, they decided to stay put, and wait and see what happened. But Zapata and de la O were soon proved right. Huerta reappointed General Robles as commander in Morelos and the south. There was not, however, any immediate large scale fighting, though some

Zapatista units again occupied a number of Mexico City suburbs.

But by the middle of April, Federal troops had quietly driven the few *Zapatistas* out of the suburbs of Mexico City, and into the surrounding mountains. Then the Federals, under the command of General Robles, seized, garrisoned and fortified the state capital, Cuernavaca. The railroad line between Cuernavaca and Mexico City was reopened.

On April 21, at a banquet in the Jockey Club, given in Huerta's honour by the planters and *hacendados* of Morelos, he promised them that he would take extreme measures to wipe out *Zapatismo* by depopulating the state, and then bringing in other workers from elsewhere in Mexico to work on their *haciendas*. He would, he boasted, wipe out the *Zapatistas* 'within a month.' He admitted that the ordinary country people of Morelos were 'all *Zapatistas*.'

Meanwhile, Zapata's position in relation to the other chiefs had become stronger. They soon realised that he had been right about Huerta. Furthermore, the *peones* and *rancheros* looked upon 'Miliano', as they called him, not as a *politico* or even as the Supreme Chief of the Liberation Army of the South, but as their '*caudillo*' who did what they wanted him to do.*

At the same time, Zapata moved his headquarters back to Villa de Ayala as a permanent base, where he was assisted by Manuel Palafox, a libertarian 'intellectual' and an engineer, who had taken the place of the *Zapatista* agents still in jail in Mexico City. Palafox helped Zapata and the chiefs co-ordinate plans, and dispatch instructions to chiefs in outlying areas of the state and adjoining states.

Immediately following Huerta's declaration of war against Morelos, the Liberation Army attacked Jonacatepec. There were nearly 500 Federal troops in the town; but within thirty-six hours they had surrendered. The *Zapatistas* captured a large amount of war supplies, including 300 Maussers, some machine-guns, much ammunition and over 200 horses. As a gesture of goodwill — or, perhaps, as a public relations exercise — Emiliano pardoned all the Federals, including

---

*The situation was very similar in the Ukraine between 1918 and 1921, following the Russian Revolution, where Nestor Makhno, the commander of the Insurrectionary Army, became BAT'KO (the Little Father) to many of the peasants who were struggling against their Red, White and Nationalist enemies. Indeed, the MAKHNOVSHCHINA in the Ukraine was very similar to ZAPATISMO in southern Mexico and Morelos.

the officers and the commandant, General Higinio Aguila, a very wily old bird whom Zapata later once used as a go-between for the purchase of arms and ammunition from corrupt Federal officers.

On April 23, the *Zapatistas* struck again. They laid seige to Cuautla; and on May 1, a group led by Genovevo de la O, dynamited a troop train on the Mexico City-Cuernavaca line, killing 100 Federal soldiers. On May 5, Zapata began to attack Cuernavaca itself; but he was unable to take it quickly, so he called off the operation.

Zapata never attacked in force unless he was sure that he was in a strong position. On the other hand, he always aimed − if he knew that he was likely to be attacked − to get in first if possible; and he was, at that time, well aware that Huerta intended to wipe him and the Liberation Army out. Indeed, Zapata fought Huerta with even more determination than he had Diaz and Madero. But he was unable to drive the Federal Army completely from Morelos.

General Robles once again resumed his 'resettlement' policy. Where and when possible, he began to round up the *peones*, and ship them, in cattle trucks, to Mexico City. Many of them were then drafted into the Federal Army, and sent almost immediately to northern Mexico to fight against Villa and others who were also in revolt against Huerta. Given the opportunity, many deserted, and either joined Villa or made their way back to Morelos.

The Federal forces were not, however, strong enough to depopulate Morelos. A column would advance upon a village or a number of villages, only to find that the *peones* and *rancheros* had fled into the hills or mountains. Many of the villagers joined Zapata. The Federals would then burn down their huts and leave. The villagers would return, and start to rebuild their huts.

Nevertheless, many of the planters did lose their workers. Some, therefore, demanded that Robles be replaced, or that Huerta reinforce Robles' troops, and wipe out *Zapatismo* once and for all. In July, they came to an agreement with Huerta whereby the Ministry of the Interior would supply them with arms, ammunition and adequate guards − that is *rurales* − to protect their *haciendas*. Huerta promised to leave the planters and *hacendados* at least thirty per cent of their local work force. But none of his guarantees or promises were kept. Moreover, General Robles, on orders from Huerta, continued to round up villagers, where he could, often leaving their wives and children to fend for themselves in hastily constructed concentration camps. Robles also seized control of, and shut down, the markets of Cuautla, Cuernavaca and Jojutla, thus aggravating the food problem. In many areas Federal troops destroyed water supplies. Malaria swept the state. Also, gangs of starving women scavengers roamed the countryside. Morelense society began to disintegrate and fall apart. General Robles told an indignant Rosa King: 'I am trying to clean up your beautiful Morelos for you; what a nice place it will be once we get rid of the Morelenses . . . . . If they resist me, I shall hang them like ear-rings from the trees.' By mid-summer, 1913, he had deported about 1,200 villagers.

Huerta never made any secret of his intentions. Unlike Madero, he did not consider himself a liberal or a democrat. In fact, Huerta's rule was a military dictatorship, which was both inefficient and severely repressive. Rather than allow the ordinary people to control their own destiny, and take back what was theirs — the *ejidos* and common lands — Huerta and the Federal Army were prepared to destroy Morelos and wipe out its people. But neither the Liberation Army or the Federal Army was strong enough to defeat the other.

CHAPTER IX

PANCHO VILLA

IN JUNE, 1913, the Liberation Army 'High Command' was reorganised. A 'Revolutionary Junta of the Centre and the South of the Republic' was set up, which included Montano, Neri, Salazar and, for the first time, de la O. Zapata remained 'Supreme Chief of the Liberation Army of the South and Centre', as well as *ex-officio* president of the junta. The secretary of the junta was Palafox.

The junta issued a new list of instructions to the revolutionaries, and amended the *Plan de Ayala* by declaring that Huerta had become the usurper. 'Taxes' were to be levied on prosperous merchants and businessmen. Authority with regard to the restoration of *ejido* lands was to be decentralised, with 'officers in the field' giving 'moral and material support' only.

Of course, things did not always work out as planned, particularly in Morelos, where General Robles was still raiding, looting and burning *pueblos*.

By July, Robles had almost 7,000 troops in Morelos and the south. Nevertheless, throughout the countryside, the *Zapatistas* still generally held sway. But more important, Huerta's campaign against Zapata and other groups was becoming far too costly. Huerta

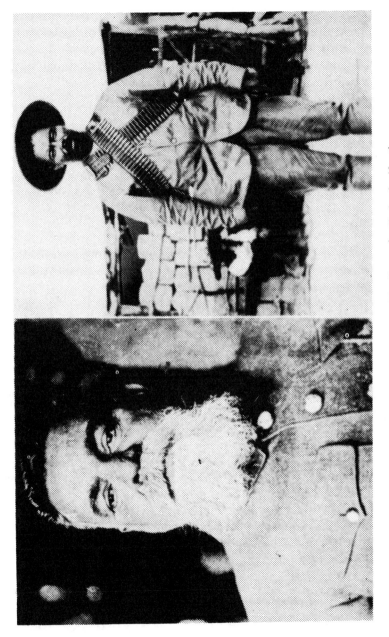

Carranza on the left and Pancho Villa, Zapata's ally in the North.

printed plenty of money, but it bought less and less. Inflation was rampant. So, by the beginning of September, General Robles was finally recalled to Mexico City. Huerta gave him two weeks' vacation; and on September 10, his vacation was lengthened indefinitely. He was then relieved of his command, and was replaced by Brigadier Adolfo Jimenez Castro. Half the Federal troops were withdrawn from Morelos and the south. Brigadier Castro took things easy. He garrisoned a couple of towns; and he even burned two villages, but in the main he and his troops just sat about drinking *pulque* and sleeping.

In late September, Zapata moved his headquarters from Villa de Ayala into Guerrero, since it was strategically better placed for extending the struggle throughout southern Mexico. On October 4, further instructions – drawn up by Palafox – were issued to the various units of the Liberation Army with the object of improving its command-structure. There were warnings against pillaging. And soldiers in combat, or on the move, were requested to remain with their own assigned units.

At the end of October, Emiliano Zapata issued a manifesto pledging that the *Zapatistas* would continue the armed struggle against the Mexican state and the *hacendados*, until the revolution had achieved profound changes in Mexican society. Their aim, he said, was to provide for economic liberty, improved living standards, and 'a just social and political order, and a free, peaceful, and civilised future' for all in Mexico.

Once in their new headquarters, Zapata, and his advisors, worked out their plan of campaign. They would 'march' the main Liberation Army force first to the railhead of Iguala, and then on to the Guerrero state capital of Chilpancingo. Mendoza, Neri and de la O would make simultaneous attacks on the remaining Federal forces in Morelos. Other chiefs would make diversionary attacks on Federal troops in southern Puebla. Following the co-ordinated attacks on Guerrero, Morelos and Puebla, Zapata would capture Chilpancingo. If successful, the Liberation Army would make a final, massive drive towards Mexico City and destroy Huerta for good and all.

Throughout November and December, the *Zapatistas* built up their forces. Chief after chief throughout the southern states rallied to their banner and the *Plan de Ayala*. Many Federal soldiers deserted to the Liberation Army. The year, which began so well for Huerta, ended badly for him.

By the end of February 1914, the Liberation Army had captured most of the towns north of Guerrero, except the state capital, Chilpancingo. Zapata, therefore, called a junta of all the chiefs at Cuetzala, where they worked out their tactics for the final assault on Chilpancingo. On March 9, the troops of Julian Blanco (a former *Maderista* who had at one time fought Zapata) took up positions south of the state capital; and to the north stood the forces of another chief, Heliodoro Castillo. On March 12, Emiliano Zapata arrived with 2,000 reinforcements from Puebla and Morelos, and set up a temporary headquarters at Tixtla, a few kilometres to the northeast.

Zapata's combined forces now totalled nearly 8,000, against 1,500 Federals under the command of the infamous General Luis G. Carton. Two days later, on Zapata's orders, a siege closed up the city. The government could send no more reinforcements. Moreover, in Morelos, the Federal garrison at Jojutla mutinied.

On March 26, Zapata prepared for a final assault, but a rather impetuous chief named Encarnacion Diaz arrived on the scene with a small force of horsemen, disregarded Zapata's instructions and rode his men straight into the Federal lines. Emiliano decided that, despite such adventurist tactics, the Liberation Army must support them. They attacked; and early the next morning, the city was in *Zapatista* hands. General Carton, with about 500 Federals, managed to escape along the Acapulco road, pursued by a force under the command of Julian Blanco. They were soon caught, and surrendered to the *Zapatistas*. All the ordinary ranks, most of whom were conscripts, were set free — and many of them joined the Liberation Army. All the Federal officers were taken to Zapata's Tixtla Headquarters, where they were court martialled. Almost all of them were released, but a few, including Carton, were found guilty of incendiarism, and were executed in Chipancingo's plaza.

At Tixtla, Zapata called a junta of chiefs in Guerrero. And in accordance with article thirteen of the *Plan de Ayala*, they elected a governor — General Salgado — of the state. He did not stay in the state very long, but after purging the old *Porfirista* bureaucrats, moved north with his forces towards Mexico City. Genovevo de la O thrust deep into Mexico State; Francisco Mendoza and Eufemio Zapata attacked and occupied *haciendas* in Puebla, but Emiliano returned to Morelos.

By the beginning of May, 1914, almost all the villages, *haciendas* and towns in Morelos and the south were safely in *Zapatista* hands. The only remaining Federal stronghold was Cuernavaca. Zapata decided, in late May, to surround the city. He cut off all supplies. He then laid seige to it. Near the end of June, the *Zapatista* assault began. On the seventh day of the assault, Cuernavaca was so near to capture that the commander — General Romero — was on the point of ordering a general evacuation. But early in July, a powerful relief column of Federals fought its way through to the besieged city; and General Ojeda, a *Porfirista* veteran, took over its defence. Once again Zapata was compelled to fall back upon siege tactics.

To put an end to the civilian suffering in Cuernavaca, Zapata promptly offered General Ojeda terms of 'honourable surrender,' which included the right to keep his sword and to entrain his troops under safe conduct to Mexico City. But Ojeda was a stubborn military egoist. He gave Zapata the customary answer: 'We fight to the last cartridge, and the last man.' The now almost defunct government of Victoriano Huerta sent a number of freight trains with supplies. Not one got through. Two were taken outright by the *Zapatistas*; and when the third arrived at Tres Marias, the Federal column sent to protect it, and transport the freight by mule-train to Cuernavaca, deserted *en masse* to the Liberation Army.

Zapata let the civilian population know that all those who wished to leave the city would find food and protection in his encampments. Most of the population accepted his offer.

The half-empty city, with its dead, dying and Federal defenders, and the remaining civilians, awaited the final assault. General Ojeda, realising that he could hold out no longer, at last ordered an immediate evacuation. He could not retreat north, for the Cima Divide was held by the *Zapatistas*. His only alternative was a desperate march southwards, and then westwards, over the Sierra de Chalma, to Toluca in the State of Mexico. Taking the remaining women and children as a 'shield' for his troops, Ojeda began his retreat southwards. In dense darkness of a torrential night rainstorm, the Federal rearguard proceeded to blow up their abandoned stores and supplies. Unaware that Ojeda had surrounded his column with civilian hostages, the *Zapatistas* attacked the retreating Federals. Only after daybreak did Zapata realise what had happened. Of the 6,000 troops and hostages who had left Cuernavaca that night, only 600 survived.

The northward advance of other Liberation Army forces towards Mexico City had slowed down because of a shortage of ammunition, though very little ammunition was needed to take the capital, and by the end of June small mounted groups reached the southern suburbs. Meanwhile, in the city itself, Huerta's dictatorship was rapidly drawing to a close. And in Morelos, Emiliano Zapata, the man who did not want power, position or privilege, had not only won a state: he was, to all intents and purposes, the *jefe maximo*, the Supreme Chief, of all Mexico south of Mexico City.

IN assuming power, Huerta and his backers hoped to put the clock back. The Federal Army, most of the *hacendados*, all the *Porfirista* elements and the Catholic Church rallied to his support. He managed to get large donations from a number of bankers; and the Church lent him one million pesos — and the hierarchy instructed priests to preach sermons extolling the 'virtues' of the new leader.

Busts and portraits of Don Porfirio Diaz, removed from public buildings during Madero's presidency, were replaced. Huerta intended to 'save the nation' at all costs. He would be Mexico's Cromwell, said his supporters. Others, less polite, called him *El Chacal* — The Jackal. Yet once in power, Huerta did not know how to keep it. When his erstwhile supporters became reluctant, he would remind them of the number of trees in Chapultepec Park suitable for hanging purposes. His printing presses, when he was short of money, printed more for him.

Huerta conducted the nation's business at the oddest times, and in the most peculiar places. He was rarely found in the National Palace, and never in Congress. His favourite haunt was El Globo, a fashionable tearoom, where he would sit for hours drinking cognac, and playing 'games' with the waitresses. Most of his cabinet meetings were held in El Colon bar with the inevitable *copita* in front of him. He smoked the cheapest cigarettes he could buy; and he was a regular user of marijuana. Yet Huerta was personally fearless. He was shaved daily by a barber whose brother he had had condemned to death before a firing squad.

Such was the man who — when he was reasonably sober — ruled Mexico!

While Zapata was slowly but inexorably winning in Morelos and the south, Huerta's 'Constitutionalist' enemies were doing likewise in the north of the country. Huerta's main opponents in northern Mexico were Venustiano Carranza, Alvaro Obregon and Doroteo Arango — universally known as Francisco 'Pancho' Villa — a bandit who became a general.*

*'Perhaps of all professional bandits in the western world, he was the one with the most distinguished revolutionary career'. (E.J.Hobsbawm, BANDITS, London, 1972, p.105).

Venustiano Carranza was tall and big-bellied, had a large white beard parted in the middle and wore blue-tinted glasses. He was unemotional, aloof, autocratic, patriarchal and cruel. He came from a wealthy and very conservative landowning *creole* family. He had served as a senator in the Diaz government for twelve years, but became a somewhat reluctant disciple of Madero in 1910. He had, however, never been an active revolutionist. Then, to everyone's surprise, he assumed the leadership of the anti-Huerta rebellion in the north. He published a vague and rambling document — *Plan de Guadalupe* — in which he proclaimed himself 'First Chief' of the Constitutionalist Army; not that there was anything particularly constitutional about the Constitutionalists. Carranza was convinced that he alone could save Mexico from Huerta.

Alvaro Obregon was part Spanish and part Irish. He was, therefore, a *creole*. His parents, though not *peones*, were quite poor for *creoles*. But Obregon went to school until he was thirteen — and was also influenced by an older brother, who was a schoolteacher and a freethinker. He started work as an apprentice mechanic on a local *hacienda*. Life was not easy for young Alvaro. He was generally easy-going. But he had a phenomenal memory. And, after working hard for some years, he became a *ranchero*. Obregon took no part in the *Maderista* rebellion, though he considered himself something of a libertarian, and sympathised with Madero. He did not particularly want to fight anyone; yet when Orozco rebelled against Madero in 1912, Obregon raised a company of 300 men, and became their commander. And when Huerta demanded the allegiance of all the states, Obregon was one of the first to support the anti-*Huertista* governor of Sonora. In his very first battle, Obregon displayed both skill and daring.

Pancho Villa was a *mestizo*, and was very slightly negroid. His family were *campesinos* from the state of Durango. They were very poor. Villa never went to school, and only learnt to read and write late in life. At sixteen, he became an outlaw. It was said that a local *hacendado*, or his son, had raped young Villa's sister — a quite common practice in those days — and that the rebellious Pancho had killed him. Anyway, Villa escaped and joined an outlaw band of cattle rustlers. Villa soon became a skilled horseman, backwoods' butcher and gun-slinger. He was a very big man. He was famed for his bravery, but better known for his short temper and 'outbursts of unspeakable cruelty.' Yet, Villa was overwhelmed by the 'goodness' of Francisco Madero. Early in 1913, Villa, who had been living in El Paso in

92

Texas, crossed the border with eight followers, and resolved to destroy Huerta – the man who he said had murdered his 'good friend' Madero. Shortly after, agents of Carranza contacted him. Villa soon developed into a military commander instead of just a leader of outlaws and gun-slingers.

THROUGHOUT the Spring and Summer of 1913, Obregon and Villa recruited their armies, and built up their supplies. Huerta largely ignored their efforts, though he did attempt to fortify a number of towns, cities and railroad junctions in the north of the country.

At the end of September, Villa, with a formidable force of over 8,000 men called the Division of the North, attacked the Federals at Torreon which he captured on October 2. The supplies of arms and ammunition, captured from the Federal Army, were enormous. They even included a hospital train, complete with sixty doctors.

By December, Huerta's dictatorship was already beginning to crumble. The economic situation was in a state of utter chaos. Huerta closed down all the banks. No one paid any bills. In a desperate attempt to increase the size of the Federal Army, Huerta began to press-gang men. Many were taken from their homes, cinemas and bullfights. Most of them had to be locked in their barracks or transport trains. It was not surprising, therefore, that Villa soon controlled the whole of the Chihuahua state, that Obregon had taken control of Sonora and that another Constitutionalist general, Pablo Gonzalez, was on the point of taking both Monterrey and Saltillo. All that Huerta could hope for was recognition of his regime by the United States. But this was not forthcoming. Indeed, the new American president, Woodrow Wilson, gave active support and sold arms to the Constitutionalists.

Villa captured Ojinaga early in January, 1914, and was in Chihuahua City at the beginning of March; Obregon's forces were moving down the Pacific Coast towards Mexico City and Gonzalez's forces threatened the Gulf Coast ports.

But things did not go entirely smoothly for Carranza, the 'First Chief' of the Constitutionalist forces. Relations with Villa were already beginning to strain. Villa demanded five million pesos from Carranza to finance his offensive against Huerta. Carranza said that he had not got the money – so, Villa printed his own. Of course, Villa's money had no value, except where people were obliged to accept it by force of arms.

In spite of his alleged shortage of funds, Villa continued to build up his army. Torreon had been recaptured by the Federals; and Huerta had garrisoned it with more than 10,000 troops. On March 16, Villa moved his forces south. Telephone and telegraph communications were cut, and trains and automobiles were forbidden to leave Chihuahua in case their occupants should give warning to the Federal Army in Torreon.

The Division of the North left Chihuahua in ten trains, including two construction trains, the hospital train and two trains loaded with artillery and cannons. The cavalry also travelled by train. Pancho Villa's army, just twelve months after his entry into the country with only eight men, was now the most powerful military machine in the entire history of Mexico . . . .

On April 3, after a number of bloody encounters, in which the Division of the North suffered over 1,000 killed and 2,000 wounded, Torreon fell to Villa. His army now controlled an area about the size of Spain. Thousands of Federal troops deserted; and many joined the Division of the North, which continued to move south, but at a somewhat slower pace. The road to Mexico City was now open.

Over on the Pacific Coast, Obregon's forces continued to make progress against less opposition. In the east, Gonzalez's Constitutionalist forces by-passed Monterrey and Saltillo, and drove on south towards the oil port of Tampico. On April 24, Monterrey fell to the Constitutionalists; and on May 10, Gonzalez captured Tampico.

Huerta's position was now almost hopeless.

At the same time, however, relations between Carranza and Villa became further strained. Villa was preparing to advance against the mining town of Zacatecas, when Carranza arrived at his headquarters. Villa welcomed him with parades and a banquet. But Carranza had no intention of letting Villa have his own way. He ordered him not to continue south towards Mexico City, but to capture isolated Federal-held strongholds like Saltillo. Reluctantly, Villa agreed. Carranza was, of course, quite aware that if Villa and his army – now nearly 20,000-strong – arrived in the capital before Obregon there would be little chance of him becoming president.

Villa soon captured Saltillo without firing a shot. And, ignoring Carranza, he again began to move his massive army south. In the bloodiest episode in the whole history of the Mexican revolution, Villa attacked Zacatecas with his entire Division of the North. It soon fell. But Villa's forces were now short of coal and other supplies – and Carranza knew it. He, therefore, diverted supplies to Obregon. Carranza continued to wait for Obregon who, on July 6, captured

Guadalara to the west of Mexico City.

On July 15, Huerta submitted his resignation to the Chamber of Deputies. Two days later, he boarded the German cruiser, *Dresden*, at Puerto Mexico and, like Don Porfirio Diaz before him, went into exile.

WHILE Villa and the Constitutionalist armies were winning battles, and capturing towns and cities with a great loss of life in the north of the country, *Zapatista* forces were right at the gates of Mexico City. Why did they not attack? Why did they merely assemble about 4,000 horsemen — and then stay put? Why did they not take the city, and chase Huerta out themselves? Carranza and the Constitutionalists were asking these questions.

The *Zapatistas* were, of course, short of ammunition. But Henry Bamford Parkes probably comes near to the truth when he writes:

'Carranza and Villa were the only chieftains whose objective was that traditional prize of the conquerors, the National Palace. Yet there was a third party in the field, a party whose aims were more genuinely revolutionary, and who would one day be recognised as having been the purest embodiment of the asperations of the Mexican masses — the Liberation Army of the South whose general and organising genius was Emiliano Zapata. From his headquarters in the hills above Cuernavaca, Zapata gradually extended his operations towards the seacoast — through the southern mountains which had been the realm of Morelos and Vincent Guerrero and Juan Alvarez — and into Puebla and the State of Mexico, and the valley of the Federal District itself. And where ever the *Zapatistas* went, they burnt the *haciendas* and murdered the administrators and divided the lands among the *peones*. They were never an army (in the real sense of the word . . .), for they spent their time ploughing and reaping their newly won lands and took up arms only to repel invasion; they were an insurgent people. As long as they held their lands, they scarcely cared who occupied the National Palace or called himself president.'

The majority of *Zapatistas* had disbanded, and were, once again, working in the fields or rebuilding their recently-destroyed huts. Many felt that they had achieved their objective, and had won their revolution; though Emiliano Zapata was still convinced that there was a long and bitter struggle ahead. He conceived the revolution in much broader terms.

95

CHAPTER X

THE CONVENTION

CARRANZA ordered Obregon to advance upon Mexico City as fast as possible. Meanwhile Eduardo N. Iturbide, the governor of the Federal District, had been left in charge of 'law and order' in the city. Carranza had, at least for the time being, successfully neutralised Villa and the Division of the North. But he was still worried — needlessly as it turned out — about Zapata and the Liberation Army of the South. He, therefore, accepted the Federals' offer to remain at their positions in Mexico City until Obregon's forces arrived. Zapata was infuriated by the decision.

By August 9, Obregon reached the railroad station of Teoloyucan, just over thirty kilometres to the north of the capital. Two days later, a delegation of Federals, headed by Iturbide, arrived at Obregon's camp to make arrangements for handing the city over to the Constitutionalists. Carranza also arrived at the station by train from Saltillo. On August 13, the Treaty of Teoloyucan was signed. And the next day the Federal Army officially gave up the city. On August 15, Obregon and his forces entered Mexico City. He immediately proclaimed martial law. He went to the National Palace, and took possession in Carranza's name. Three days later, Venustiano Carranza made his triumphal entry. All the Constitutionalist generals — except, of course, General Pancho Villa! — arrived and occupied the city's finest mansions.

Once in the capital, Carranza took the law into his own hands. He shut down the railway to Veracruz. He snubbed the foreign diplomats, dissolved the National Academy, refused to reconvene Congress, closed the courts, disarmed the city's police, jailed all the Catholic priests his largely anti-clerical troops could find and kept all administrative authority in his own hands. He assumed the rather verbose title of 'First Chief in Charge of the Executive Power.' And he declared Huerta's currency worthless — which it was anyway — proclaiming his own money, which he was printing by the hundreds of millions of pesos, as the only legal tender. Old scores were settled. Constitutionalist troops went on the rampage, and many houses were looted.

Obregon began to attempt to patch up the differences between himself and Carranza on the one hand, and Villa, and to some extent Zapata, on the other. Relations between Obregon and Villa were reasonably friendly at first; but later, when they met, Villa lost his temper and almost had Obregon shot. Obregon returned to Mexico City.

Carranza proceeded with his plans for a junta in October, in which neither Villa's Division of the North nor Zapata's Liberation Army of the South were to be invited. Carranza's attitude, nevertheless, worried a number of his supporters, including Obregon. They, therefore, decided that all anti-*Huertista* forces, including the *Villistas* and *Zapatistas*, must be invited. So, they decided to hold a junta in Aguascalientes, half-way between Mexico City and Villa's headquarters at Chihuahua. Carranza, however, remained adamant. He said that his junta would be in Mexico City, and would be on October 1; and he refused to invite either Villa or Zapata.

On October 1, Carranza's junta did indeed meet in the Chamber of Deputies, in Mexico City. But all the 'delegates' present, except Carranza, decided that they were going on to the Aguascalientes junta anyway, since it would at least be more representative. Carranza addressed the junta, then swept out. The others prepared for their journey northwards to Aguascalientes.

NEITHER Emiliano Zapata nor the men from Morelos were prepared to accept Carranza as 'First Chief' of the revolution. And Carranza had always looked upon the *Zapatistas* as 'rabble.' *Carrancista* agents had, on a number of occasions, however, visited Zapata, hoping that he would put his forces under Carranza's command. But Constitutionalist feelers came to nothing. If Carranza would not accept the *Plan de Ayala*, then the *Zapatistas* would not recognise him. Moreover, Antonio Diaz Soto y Gama, a libertarian and a fiery orator who had become a *Zapatista* secretary, particularly warned Emiliano against the Spanish aristocrat.

It was no secret that Zapata had made contact with the *Villistas*, and the Division of the North. Indeed, one *Zapatista*, Gildardo Magana, had visited Villa previously when he was in jail in Mexico City, and had explained the *Plan de Ayala* to him. Between March and August, 1914, a number of *Villista* agents had attended Morelos juntas, and had had audiences with Zapata; but Emiliano did not officially commit himself to an alliance with General Villa. Following Obregon's entry into Mexico City, his agents also contacted the

Zapatistas, but nothing came of this either. Nevertheless, exchanges between the various Constitutionalist factions and the *Zapatistas* continued throughout August and September. But Carranza refused to consider the *Plan de Ayala* even as a basis of discussion. Zapata broke off all contact.

At the end of August, Emiliano Zapata and thirty-five chiefs met and published an important manifesto.

'The revolutionary movement has reached its culminating point, and it is time, therefore, for the country to know the truth.' proclaimed Zapata. 'The existing revolution did not make itself for the purpose of satisfying the interests of any one person, of any one group or party. The existing revolution recognises that its origins lie deeper and that it is pursuing higher aims.

The *peon* was hungry, was enduring misery, was suffering from exploitation, and if he rose in arms it was to obtain the bread that the rich denied him, to make himself master of the land that the egoistic landed proprietor kept for himself, to vindicate the dignity the slave-driver iniquitously trampled on daily. He threw himself into revolt, not to conquer illusory rights which do not feed him, but to procure land which must supply him with food and liberty.

The revolution will be brought to a happy conclusion when the people, individually and in their communities, receive back the innumerable tracts of land of which they have been despoiled by the great *hacendados*; and this great act of justice receives its complement, as those who have nothing and have had nothing, in the proportional repartition of the lands given to the dictatorship's accomplices, or of those expropriated from idle proprietors who do not chose to cultivate their heritages. Thus, there will be satisfied both the human demand for land and that apetite for liberty which is making itself felt throughout the republic as the formidable reply to the savagery of the *hacienda* òwners which has maintained, even in the twentieth century, a system which the most unfortunate serfs of the Middle Ages in Europe would hardly have endured . . . .

The country people wish to live the life of civilisation; to breath the air of liberty which, as yet, they have not known; and this they never can do while there still remain the traditional lord of the scaffold and the knife, who disposes at whim of the persons of his labours; an extortioner of wages, who annihilates them with excessive tasks, brutalises them by misery and ill-treatment, dwarfs and exhausts his race by the slow agony of slavery and enforced withering of human beings whose stomachs and empty brains are very hungry.

If the leader of the Constitutionalists considers that he has the popularity needed to stand the proof of its submission to a vote of the revolutionaries, let him submit to it without vacillation; and if the Constitutionalists really love the people and understand what they demand, let them do homage to their sovereign will, accepting with sincerity and without any reticence the *Plan de Ayala* — expropriation of the land for the sake of public utility, expropriation of the property of the people's enemies, and the restitution to the towns and the communities of that which they have been despoiled.

If that is not done, they may rest assured that the agitation of the masses will continue, that the war will go on in Morelos, Puebla, in Guerrero, in Hidalgo, in Oaxaca, in Durango, in Tlaxcala, in Chihuahua, in Michoacan, in Guanuato, In San Luis Potosi, in Tamaulipas, in Zacatecas, wherever there are lands . . . . and the great movement of the south, supported by all the country, will continue, conquering all opposition and combatting all resistance . . . .'

Such was the cry of Emiliano Zapata!

On September 8, Zapata issued from his headquarters in Cuernavaca a decree to execute article eight of the *Plan de Ayala*, whereby all landlords, planters and *hacendados* who opposed the *Plan* would have at least two-thirds of their property and land confiscated for indemifications of war. The decree said that such confiscations would apply to both urban as well as rural property. Chiefs were to initiate proceedings, and *pueblos* and municipalities were to report inventories to the *Zapatista* headquarters.

Of course, throughout Morelos and a number of other states, much of the *Plan de Ayala* had already been implemented, and had taken effect. Many of the *hacienda* lands had been taken back by the *peones*. At Cuautla, Eufemio Zapata directed that agrarian commissions of locally elected *peones* and *rancheros* should be appointed, and begin work.

Most of the Liberation Army had been disbanded — though mobilisation could, if necessary, be very rapid. Those *Zapatistas* still under arms remained where they were; but, at least, for the first time since their campaign began, the *peones* and *rancheros* of Morelos and the south had abundant stores, and arms and ammunition. The Liberation Army had over two million cartridges and even some artillery. And thousands of *Zapatistas* now owned their own rifles.

AGUASCALIENTES — Hot Waters — was a peaceful, prosperous

town of nearly 60,000 inhabitants. It had been officially declared a 'neutral' town, and was governed by a joint commission representing both Carranza and Villa. But Villa had far more influence in the area than did Carranza.

During the first week of October, the 'revolutionaries' began to arrive. The small railroad yard was jam-packed with locomotives, boxcars, cabooses and sleeping cars, each with its *jefe politico* or 'revolutionary' general. The hotels were inadequate. Local people were forced to give up their homes. Most of the Constitutionalist 'delegates' arrived from Mexico City. Pancho Villa encamped with 12,000 troops at Guadalupe, less than two hundred kilometres to the north. All the *cantinas* had been closed; but the town swarmed with armed men, their cartridge belts full of ammunition and, in the words of one observer, 'their bellies full of *tequila.*'

Alvaro Obregon was the leading Constitutionalist and *Carrancista* spokesman. On his arrival at the Convention, which was held in the Morelos Theatre, he presented the assembled 'delegates' with a special flag – the Mexican Standard, inscribed with the words 'Military Convention of Aguascalientes.' He asked all present to sign their names upon it; and those who could write, did so. Obregon then made an emotional speech, declaring that he was prepared to give up his general's insignia and, 'with a sergeant's stripes', go and fight anyone who opposed the Convention. General Chao, a *Villista*, said he would do likewise, 'as a plain soldier.' Speech followed speech in similar vein. Speeches were often punctuated by pistol shots, and applause was signified by the crashing of rifle butts on the floor. The 'delegates' were having themselves a ball.

But Emiliano Zapata had not arrived at the Convention; nor had any representative from the Liberation Army of the South.

For five days the Convention speculated on the non-arrival of Zapata. On October 12, a *Villista* delegate proposed that they formerly invite the *Zapatistas*; and four days later, General Felipe Angeles was sent to Zapata's headquarters with a verbal invitation for Zapata and the men from the south to attend the Convention as soon as possible.

On October 17, to the accompaniment of 'Viva Villa' from his supporters, Pancho Villa arrived at the Convention. He made a rather incoherent speech in which he told the audience that he was uncultured but sincere. Afterwards, he broke down and wept. Obregon stepped forward and gave his old antagonist an *abrazo.* So, Villa made another almost identical speech. He then returned to his encampment at Guadalupe, more than pleased with himself.

The same day Angeles arrived in Mexico City; and two days later, together with Alfredo Serratos and three companions, he left for Cuernavaca. On arrival, he arranged with Manuel Palafox to meet Zapata.

At noon they met. They had not met before. Zapata, never particularly demonstrative towards those whom he did not know, was surprisingly cordial towards Angeles, the former moderate *Maderista* commander in Morelos, who had now thrown in his lot with Villa and the Convention. Nevertheless, Zapata emphasised that it was not for him to decide whether or not a delegation should be sent to Aguascalientes; it was for the chiefs, as representatives of the people, to make such a decision. Emiliano, therefore, sent word that a conference of chiefs should be held as soon as possible at the Liberation Army headquarters. Zapata told Angeles that he did not intend to attend the Convention anyway. He would remain in Morelos. He also said that, personally, he would not like to see accredited *Zapatista* delegates at a meeting dominated by *Carrancistas*, even if many of them were independent *Carrancistas*. None of them had been elected, he added. Unless the Convention accepted the *Plan de Ayala*, he would not recognise it. Zapata preferred that a commission first go to Aguascalientes and then, perhaps, a full properly-elected delegation go later.

The conference at Zapata's headquarters began on October 22. Very few chiefs attended. Most of them were busy in their villages. And many were not concerned with 'national affairs', or a 'revolutionary' Convention hundreds of kilometres to the north. Of those who agreed to go, the most prominent were – quite naturally – the few *Zapatista* 'intellectuals,' who had become headquarters' secretaries and advisors. The chiefs and secretaries agreed with Zapata, and decided that they would send a commission rather than a delegation with specific instructions. The commissioners were appointed. But they were not prepared to recognise Don Venustiano Carranza as 'First Chief;' nor would they recognise the Convention unless it adopted the *Plan de Ayala*. They decided on twenty-six commisioners, including Paulino Martinez, Antonio Diaz Soto y Gama, Gildardo and Rodolfo Magana, Alfredo Serratos and Manuel Palafox. Otilio Montano was unwell and was unable to travel.

On October 23, the commisioners, together with General Angeles and his group, left by a number of cars for Mexico City. The next day they all left the capital by train. But they passed right through

Aguascalientes without stopping. Instead they went straight to Villa's headquarters at Guadalupe, where they conferred with his advisors who assured them that Villa was sympathetic towards their cause. On October 26, the *Zapatistas* arrived in Aguascalientes.

THE following morning, the *Zapatista* commisioners entered the Morelos Theatre to tumultuous applause from the 'delegates.' They entered warily, looking, according to the recording secretary, Vito Alessio Robles, 'like a troop of soldiers crossing a dangerous defile.' They were a picturesque group. Most of them wore skin-tight *charro* trousers, peasant blouses and huge sombreros, which they did not remove. The others wore typical Indian attire. None wore military uniforms. With their arrival, however, the Convention soon burst into life. And they soon threw off their wariness.

Paulino Martinez, the group's main spokesman, first took the rostrum. After praising Zapata — and Villa — he stated the *Zapatista* position. He said that they had come to the Convention not as a delegation but as a commission, to learn whether the Convention would accept the *Plan de Ayala* as its official policy with regard to the land question.

Antonio Diaz Soto y Gama then took the floor. The Convention flag stood at the left of the speaker's rostrum. Soto y Gama began to speak.

'We have come here with honourable intentions,' he said. 'We place more faith in a man's honour than a signature on a flag.' And here he grabbed the flag and shook it.

'I do not intend to sign it,' he continued.

There was a rumble from the audience. But he still held the flag.

'We are waging a great revolution against the lies of history . . . . a revolution which will expose the lie this flag represents . . . this rag . . . this standard of clerical reaction . . . '

The rumble had now turned to uproar.

'Let go of the flag! Savage! Imbecile! Barbarian! Renegade! Bastard!,' cried Colonel Vigil.

'Get off the platform!,' shouted General Villareal. 'More respect for the nation's flag'.

The assembled chiefs and generals rose to their feet, shook their fists, pounded their chests and then reached for their guns. More than one hundred pistols and rifles were pointed at the speaker.

But Soto y Gama stood his ground, arms crossed over his chest, and his head thrown back. The other *Zapatistas* drew their guns and waited. Observers in the gallery began to make for the exits. General Villareal, as interim president of the Convention, pounded his bell for order. No one seemed to hear it. After a minute or so, the noise subsided. There was no shooting. Antonio Diaz Soto y Gama looked around the building. The pistols returned to their holsters. The rifles were lowered. And when the uproar had largely abated, he said quietly: 'When you have finished, I'll go on.'

He realised, however, that he had over-stepped the mark. He explained that the flag itself was unimportant, since it was only a symbol of the state and the nation. He insisted that it was being used by the reactionaries to conceal selfish, personal ambitions. He went on to attack Carranza. He also ridiculed the men surrounding Carranza who were being rewarded with *haciendas*, money and patronage. He concluded by saying that Zapata's *Plan de Ayala* was the only true expression of the aims of the revolution.

He left the rostrum in almost complete silence. Obregon sat scowling. But Roque Gonzalez Garza, the *Villista* spokesman, said that his delegation supported Soto y Gama. And from the gallery there were shouts of 'Viva Villa!' and 'Viva Zapata!'

During the following day's debate, Paulino Martinez boasted that there were now 60,000 *Zapatistas* under arms. Immediately Obregon demanded to know why they had not captured Mexico City. Why had they waited for him, with only 23,000 men, to march over 3,500 kilometres across the republic to capture the capital, he demanded. Replied Martinez: 'You took the capital only by making compromises with the Federal Army . . . . Our hands are clean . . . . We do not compromise . . . . We have nothing but enmity for the forces of the usurper, Victoriano Huerta.'

But Martinez and the *Zapatista* commissioners were primarily concerned with winning the Convention over to, at least, a vote of support for the *Plan de Ayala*. The forty members of the *Villista* delegation had pledged their support; winning over the others — of whom the majority were *Obregonistas* or independent *Carrancistas* — would prove more difficult. Nevertheless, on October 28, after a daylong debate, much of which was acrimonious and confused, the *Zapatistas* got a small majority of the Convention to approve, 'in principle,' articles four, six, seven, nine and twelve of the *Plan de Ayala*. This was a tactical victory, if no more.

Emiliano had good reason to be pleased, as the *Zapatista* commissioners had at least made all the running once they had arrived at the Convention. Indeed, Zapata commented that 'Martinez and Soto and

Serratos made the smoke, but Palafox cooked the meat!' All the same Zapata was still wary. He wrote to Martinez on November 2, saying that he was still not in favour of the commissioners taking their seats at the Convention as 'full delegates,' unless the Convention completely repudiated, and removed, Carranza as 'First Chief.'

Unfortunately for Zapata, many of the 'delegates' wanted Carranza to attend the Convention. And on October 23, Carranza wrote a letter to the Convention; and at a closed session on October 29, Obregon revealed its contents.

Carranza indicated that if the Convention believed that his retirement would be the most effective means of restoring harmony among the 'revolutionary elements,' he would stand down subject to certain conditions; these were: the establishment of a pre-constitutional government, the retirement of General Villa and his renunciation of candidacy for the presidency and the resignation of General Zapata from command of the Liberation Army. Carranza demanded that Zapata 'leave the country.'

Anyway, the following day, the Convention accepted a formula drawn up by Obregon in which it called for the resignations of both Carranza and Villa – and thanked them for their services to the 'revolution.' But the Convention agreed to defer action on Zapata and the Liberation Army of the South 'until the *Zapatistas* were represented by regular delegates subject to the Convention's orders.' Emiliano Zapata had won another battle – a parliamentary one!

GENERAL Antonio Villareal informed Villa of the Convention's decision to relieve him of his post. Pancho said that he accepted the decision, and awaited the Convention's orders. Obregon was commissioned to inform Carranza of the decision to relieve him of his post as well.

But Carranza sensing that the Convention might call his bluff – and accept his 'offer' to retire – left Mexico City for Toluca. On his arrival he made a speech pledging to carry out the reforms promised by Madero. He then returned to Mexico City, but almost immediately set off again for San Juan Teotihuacan, where he visited the pre-Columbian pyramids. Then he, at last, arrived in Puebla. Obregon went to Puebla to try and impress upon him that he must resign, informing him that Villa had already done so. But Carranza argued that Villa had not really given up his command – he had merely turned it over to General Robles. He was, said Carranza, still the real head of the Division of the North. Carranza refused to resign.

On November 10, General Robles declared Carranza to be in a state of rebellion against the Convention 'government.' He also sent a telegram to Zapata, appealling to him to attack Carranza, who now had a very tiny army in the state of Puebla. Villa, therefore, resumed control of the Division of the North, which was renamed the Army of the Convention, and began to move south towards Mexico City. Villa telegraphed Zapata: 'The hour has come. In the morning I begin my march towards Mexico City.' But Obregon had changed his mind. He said that he would not abandon Carranza to aid a man like Villa. He declared war on Pancho. He had less than 3,000 men. After returning to Mexico City, he hurriedly left again with his little army for Veracruz, where Carranza was now in residence.

The *Carrancista* delegates to the Convention made their way to Veracruz, the *Villistas* joined Pancho for his march on the capital, the *Zapatistas* returned to Morelos and the south, the 'independents' voted to adjourn until Villa had captured Mexico City, and the so-called Convention government moved to San Luis Potosi, also hoping to establish itself in the capital later.

Civil war was soon to break out again . . . .

CHAPTER XI

ZAPATA MEETS VILLA

AS the *Obregonistas* evacuated Mexico City, the worthy bourgeois citizens of the capital awaited the arrival of, first, the *Zapatistas* and then the *Villistas* with fear and trepidation.

The barbarities of the *Carrancista* occupation in August were still fresh in their minds. Moreover, the *Zapatistas* – dark little men with large cartridge belts and sharp *machetes* – had been painted in the most lurid colours, as savage Indians, in the popular press. On November 23, *El Imparcial*, mouthpiece of reaction under Diaz, Madero and Huerta, came out with deep black borders and banner headlines, warning the citizens of a reign of 'rape and loot and massacre', which was about to descend upon them.

Late in the evening of November 24, the first small contingents of the Liberation Army filtered into the southern parts of the city. They entered quietly, almost embarrassedly. The next morning, more arrived. Altogether there were about 10,000 of them. In their cotton, and often ragged, clothes, some wearing sandals and others bare-footed, they shuffled along in most unmilitary columns, and on horseback. There was none of the bravado of previous occupying armies. There was neither the blaring of bugles, nor the beating of drums. Only the occasional mournful sound of a bullhorn trumpet could be heard. And there was no firing of guns into the air. Unlike other victorious armies of the Mexican revolution, the *Zapatistas* conserved their ammunition. Uncertain of themselves, or their role in the capital, they did not loot or plunder. There was no requisitioning of mansions, or of automobiles. And there was very little stealing of horses. For the most part, the *Zapatistas* were humble village folk accustomed to the stern ethics of their *pueblos.*

Many of the *Zapatistas* wandered through the streets of the capital, almost like children, knocking upon doors — many of which had been hastily barred or boarded up - asking for food. Due to the haste of the occupation and, to some extent lack of proper organisation, the *Zapatistas* found themselves short of food. They also lacked money. What could they do? They would not steal. So they asked. Some begged for a peso to buy a cup of coffee, but would not accept more than one, saying one was enough. Others would shuffle awkwardly into the cafes and restaurants, awed by the smart waitresses as much as the waitresses were, at least at first, afraid of them. On leaving a few of the *Zapatistas* would pay not in some useless paper money, but in silver pesos.

Unlike the *Carrancistas*, the *Zapatistas* did not execute any priests (though many of them were not strictly Christians), or close down the churches. Some even marched behind the banner of the dark Virgin of Guadalupe. Others wore religious medals or love charms and amulets against the Evil Eye.

The Liberation Army of the South took over the duties of policing the city; and the former chief of police later reported that there was not a single incident of disorder during the *Zapatista* occupation. Mexico City was calmer, quieter, and better controlled than since the days of Don Porfirio Diaz.

Eufemio Zapata and his contingent, including their horses, went to the National Palace and occupied dingy quarters at the rear. In twos and threes, they explored the great halls, their sandal-clad feet moving uneasily over the soft carpets. They stared in wonderment at the paintings, statuary and silk draperies. Eufemio, however, declared that he would burn the *silla presidencial*, thinking it was Carranza's saddle instead of the presidential chair.* But the chair was left undisturbed and undamaged by the *Zapatistas*, as was everything

*The word SILLA signifies both saddle and chair.

else in the National Palace.

With obvious pleasure, the *Zapatistas* did take over one building: the one which housed the offices and plant of *El Imparcial*. They appointed Octavio Paz and Conrado Soto y Gama as editors, changed the name to *El Nacion*, and printed it under *Zapatista* control for five consecutive days.

On November 26, Emiliano Zapata arrived, quite unobtrusively, in Mexico City by train from Cuernavaca. He refused to occupy one of the great mansions along the Paseo de la Reforma, as had all successful and many not-so-successful generals before him. Nor did he go to the National Palace. Instead, he took a room in a cheap, small railway hotel in the Calle Moneda, just by the suburban station of San Lazaro. He made no proclamations; and he issued no decrees. Reluctantly, he answered journalists' questions.

'The Liberation Army of the South holds and controls Mexico City,' said Zapata. 'But neither I nor the army intend to stay in the city . . . . I plan to return to Morelos, and await the arrival of General Villa and the Convention Army . . . . Yes . . . I am in general support of the Aguascalientes Convention, and its provisional president, General Eulalio Gutierrez. . . . '

On November 28, two days after his arrival in Mexico City, Zapata returned to Cuernavaca in Morelos.

By December 1, Villa and his Convention Army reached Tacuba, a suburb just northwest of the capital. Pancho intended to occupy Mexico City; but he would not make the same mistake of previous generals who attempted to defy or ignore Zapata. Villa wanted to meet Emiliano first.

Eulalio Gutierrez, the interim president, arrived by car in the capital the day after Villa had encamped on the *llanos*. Gutierrez first visited Eufemio Zapata in the National Palace. Villa dictated a letter to Zapata in Cuernavaca, in which he invited Emiliano to meet him in Mexico City, to give him an *abrazo*, and discuss matters of importance. He promised Zapata that he would be quite safe with him. But Emiliano Zapata, displaying his usual caution, insisted that their meeting be in the *pueblo* of Xochimilco to the southwest of Mexico City. Xochimilco was famous for its flowers, fruits and Aztec floating gardens. But, more important, it was also in *Zapatista* territory.

Villa agreed to meet Zapata there on December 4. Neither man had previously met.

Early on Friday morning, December 4, Villa and a small escort of

107

dorados set out on horseback for Xochimilco, forty kilometres from his headquarters at Tacuba, carefully skirting the centre of Mexico City, which lay between Tacuba and Xochimilco to the south.

ZAPATA carefully planned his meeting with Villa. Xochimilco was decorated with flowers and coloured streamers. There was the town band, and a choir of children. With Emiliano was Otilio Montano, the village schoolteacher who had helped Zapata with the drafting of the *Plan de Ayala*, and all the other *Zapatista* secretaries. Also present were Emiliano's brother, Eufemio, who had returned from Mexico City, his sister, Jesucita, his little son, Nicolas, and his cousin, Amador Salazar.

Villa and his escort arrived on the outskirts of Xochimilco exactly at noon. A party of *Zapatistas* stood in parade formation on either side of the street. Large crowds from Mexico City had already arrived. As Villa appeared suddenly at the head of the street, accompanied by his *dorados*, every gun went smartly to salute. They received a great, and noisy, welcome from the crowd. There were shouts of 'Viva Villa.' Then the band struck up, and the children began to sing. 'So many were the bouquets,' said Pancho afterwards, 'that our men could not carry them.' Villa and his party dismounted. Serafin Robles, on behalf of the Liberation Army, stepped forward to greet Villa; and Otilio Montano delivered a brief and formal speech of welcome.

Villa listened rather impatiently. *'Gracias, senores, muchisimas gracias.'* And then asked: 'But where is my *companero*?'.

Montano pointed down the narrow village street, and led Villa towards the school house, outside which Zapata was standing. As Villa walked down the street, the band played the famous revolutionary tune, *La Cucaracha*. Montano introduced Villa to Zapata. The two men exchanged *abrazos*. They walked arm-in-arm into the school, and upstairs into a large room on the first floor. In the room there was a very large oval table and a number of chairs.

Villa and Zapata could not have looked more different . . . .
Villa, tall, robust and ruddy-faced, was dressed fairly presentably for once. He wore a large, loose, heavy brown sweater, a bright coloured scarf, khaki military trousers, puttees and riding boots, and an English tropical pith helmet. Zapata, dark, short and slim, was far better turned out. He wore a short black jacket, tight black *charro* trousers with silver buttons down the outside seam of each leg, a

brilliant lavendar-coloured shirt with a light blue, silk hankerchief; short, black, sharp-toed, high-heeled, Spanish style boots and a massive black, wide-brimmed *sombrero* completely shading his eyes. He alternately used a white silk hankerchief with a green border, and one with all the colours of the rainbow. He had two large gold rings on the fingers of his left hand. He was the smartest man in all Mexico. Zapata's sister was less impressive; though altogether, she had about twelve rings — mostly of cheap silver — on the fingers of both hands. Zapata's son, Nicolas, wore a pair of typical Indian, loose-fitting white cotton trousers, and a colourful shirt also of the same material.

Villa sat down at the table, and Zapata sat on his left. At Villa's right was Paulino Martinez; then Leon Canova, and then Zapata's sister, and on her right young Nicolas. Eufemio Zapata sat on Emiliano's left. Other *Zapatistas* and *Villistas* sat around the big table. The room soon filled up with people. The band stayed in the corridor, but made it difficult for anyone to hear what was being said. Fortunately, after a short while the band gave up, and left the building.

For almost half-an-hour the two generals sat in embarrassed silence, exchanging occasional rambling, almost incoherent, insignificant remarks and comments, and leaving most of the discussion to others. Zapata seemed expressionless, except for his eyes which were almost hidden by his *sombrero* anyway. But he was watching Villa all the time. At last Villa began to attack Carranza. Immediately the mood changed.

Said Villa: 'I was always worried . . . . being forgotten . . . . I had an obligation to the revolution . . . . Carranza is a man so shameless . . . . He was taking over the revolution while I waited.'

'I have said to all of you . . . . I always said that Carranza is a son of a bitch,' interjected Zapata.

Villa then damned men who slept on soft beds, were always going to banquets and knew nothing of the people and their suffering.

'Such men were the people's scourge,' added Emiliano.

Now and then, Palafox, Serratos and Garza joined in. Zapata asked Villa about battles in the north of the country, appearing to know more about Villa's campaigns that Villa did about those of the *Zapatistias,*

There then followed an informal discussion about the *ejidos* and the land problem.

'The people,' observed Emiliano, 'loved the land. They still don't believe it when you tell them that it is now their land. They think it is a dream. But when they see others growing things on the land, they say that they will demand land, and plant on it.'

'And,' replied Villa: 'Now they will see that it is the people who rule, and they will see who their friends are . . . . I believe there is going to be another better life, and if not — I have forty thousand Mausers, seventy-seven cannon, and sixteen million cartridges. . . . '

Emiliano Zapata called for a bottle of cognac, and poured out two large tumblers' full.. Pancho, a life-long teetotaler, eyed them suspiciously and asked for a glass of water. Zapata raised his glass. Villa changed his mind, and rejected the water. He, too, raised his glass, saying: '*Companero*, I accept this drink solely for the pleasure of joining you, for the truth is I never drink liquor.' He drank it all straight down. Then his face reddened, and he began to splutter. Tears rolled down his cheeks. He asked for water again.

'Well, here I am,' he gasped. 'I came to meet the true men of the people.'

'I congratulate myself for meeting a man who truly knows how to fight,' responded Zapata.

'I've been at it for twenty-two years,' said Villa.

'And I since the age of eighteen,' replied Zapata.

A glass of water was placed before Villa. But turning towards Zapata, he said: 'Wouldn't you like the water?'

'No, go ahead and drink it,' said Zapata.

The band had now returned to the corridor, and conversation was, once again, almost impossible.

The discussion broke up. Villa and Zapata wanted to talk about more immediate matters. So, they and Palafox retired to another, quieter, smaller room. First, they got down to the business of planning the campaign against Carranza in Veracruz. Villa promised to supply Zapata with much-needed equipment, including a number of cannons. At Villa's request, they also made plans for a triumphal entry into Mexico City of both the Convention Army and the Liberation Army of the South, in a military parade, two days later, on Sunday, December 8. Pancho Villa then brought up the delicate subject of two men whom he and Emiliano wanted executed. Zapata asked Villa to deliver to him Guillerno Garcia Aragon, a renegade *Zapatista*; and Villa demanded of Zapata that he hand over one of his secretaries, Paulino Martinez, who was in fact in the building. Villa wanted Martinez shot because he had criticised Madero — whom Villa considered had been a saint! — in the Cuernavaca *Zapatista* newspaper,

Le Voz de Juarez. Zapata, however, refused to hand Martinez over. But both Aragon and Martinez were soon to die.

After about half-an-hour Villa and Zapata adjourned. A luncheon had been prepared — with corn, beans, chillies, roast pork and kid, and, of course, plenty of *pulque* and beer. The feast was hearty with comradeship and bawdy humour — largely at the expense of 'the old cockroach', Carranza, and his henchmen. Once again, the local band provided the music. Marciano Silver played his guitar and sang *Adelita*, and Pancho's *dorados*, not to be outdone, broke into a roaring version of *La Cucaracha*. Zapata offered Villa a cigar, but he refused it. Toasts were drunk, pledging comradeship in a common effort against Carranza and Obregon. Villa made his usual speech about being uncultured and uneducated; and affirmed his concern for the poor. Martinez, not knowing that Villa wanted him executed, also spoke, praising Zapata — and Villa. Zapata said nothing. He just watched and listened.

After the meal, Villa and his party returned to their headquarters. Zapata and his aides began to prepare for the parade in Mexico City.

CHAPTER XII

CONQUERED CAPITAL

EARLY on Sunday morning over 30,000 *Zapatistas*, with Emiliano at their head, left Xochimilco for Mexico City. They were armed with rifles and *machetes*, and many had heavy cartridge belts crossing their chests. A few wore swords. None wore military uniforms. They were a people in arms. They had come from Morelos, Guerrero, Puebla, Oaxava and Hidalgo. At San Angel and Mixcoa, on the way into the city, they were joined by others, many wearing *charro* suits and enormous cartwheel *sombreros*.

Once again, Zapata was spectacular. He wore a deerskin jacket, elaborately embroidered with silk and gold thread, the emblem of the Mexican eagle emblazoned on the back. He wore black *charro* trousers with silver buttons, and a splendid, twenty-ounce white *sombrero*, also worked in gold. And he carried a sword. He was riding his stallion, Relampago.

Somewhat later, Villa rode out at the head of the Convention Army of about 40,000 men, from his base at Tacuba. Unlike the *Zapatistas*, Villa's troops mainly wore uniforms — old Federal Army ones — and

111

marched or rode in military order. Villa wore a dark blue uniform and high leather leggings.

The two armies met in the Calzada de la Veronica, and formed into an enormous column. At the head Villa, with Zapata on his left, rode with a small cavalry escort of *Villistas* and *Zapatistas*. They moved down the Paseo de la Reforma towards the city centre and the National Palace. The *Zapatista* foot-soldiers came after Villa and Zapata and their escort, shuffling along; then came the *Zapatista* horsemen on their small, but fast, horses. The *Villistas*, marching and riding in order, followed them.

The ordinary people of Mexico City welcomed them with flowers and bouquets. Vast crowds massed along the Paseo de la Reforma all the way from Chapultepec to Alameda sending up roaring cheers — 'Viva Villa! Viva Zapata!' Mexico's *peone* army, shouting *'tierra y libertad!'*, marched victoriously through the capital. To the ceaseless thunder of drums, blaring brass bands and the braying of bullhorns, Mexico City was on parade.

The huge column moved through the city, across the north side of the Zocalo to the front of the National Palace. Villa and Zapata dismounted, and then took positions beside the interim president, Eulalio Gutierrez, on the balcony to review the parade, which continued until five in the afternoon.

After the parade, Villa and Zapata went into the National Palace; and, together with their aides and secretaries, they entered the presidential suite. The photographers prepared their cameras. Standing before the highly-ornate gilt presidential chair, Villa invited Zapata to sit in it. But Zapata replied: 'It would be better to burn it, for I have seen that everybody who has sat in this chair has become an enemy of the people.' Villa had no objection to sitting in it. The photographers were now ready. Villa sat in the presidential chair, his military cap resting on his knee. He posed for the photographers. Then, another, much smaller chair, was placed on his left side.

Zapata reluctantly agreed to sit in it, crossed his legs, and placed his enormous *sombrero* on his knee. Villa smiled at the camera; Zapata looked bored and uneasy. Other *Villistas* and *Zapatistas* crowded round. Their picture was taken . . . . for posterity.

Later that evening, Gutierrez held a banquet for Villa, Zapata, the other 'revolutionary' generals, ministers of the newly-formed Convention government, foreign diplomats and those businessmen who were still in the capital. It was a grand affair.

Mrs. Leone B. Moats, the American woman who was living in

The historical meeting in the National Palace, December, 1914. Seated, L-R, Tomas Urbina, Pancho Villa, Emiliano Zapata, unknown Zapatista, Rodolfo Fierro, in a hat, is standing on the right.

Mexico City at the time, and who attended the banquet, remembers an incident concerning Emiliano Zapata and his wife, who was also present. Says Mrs. Moats:

'General Zapata had placed his wife next to him. Never having eaten at a table before, she proceeded quite naturally to push back her chair, put her plate on her lap and eat with her fingers. The Spanish Minister was sitting next to her. It took quick action on his part to get his coat tails well tucked under before they became a mass of grease spots. Someone asked Zapata why he had placed his wife, instead of one of the other ladies, beside him. He answered in surprise: "But I know my wife, and what do you think I could talk about to the wife of a diplomat?".'

Throughout the banquet, both Villa and Zapata were ill-at-ease. They did not enjoy the formal atmosphere. Gutierrez was uneasy too. He did not trust Villa. But, more important, he did not know what to make of Zapata. Yet he was completely dependent upon them both.

The next morning, Villa and Zapata visited Gutierrez in the National Palace. They informed him of their plans for crushing Carranza and Obregon. Villa and the Convention Army would drive northeast from Mexico City, and then southeast towards Veracruz; Zapata and the Liberation Army would push towards the coast through the state of Puebla. This was Villa's plan, which Zapata appeared to accept. And of Zapata, Mrs. Moats observes: 'Zapata was afraid of the city; a countryman by instinct, with a hill man's sagacity, he betook to his private train, and did not rest until it was side-tracked well out of town.'

This was largely true. On the other hand, he intended to direct operations against the *Carrancistas* and *Obregonistas* in Puebla. Nevertheless, had Emiliano Zapata been anyone else, he could – and probably would – have stayed on in Mexico City, and become president and virtual dictator of Mexico. It would not have been too difficult for him to have installed himself in the National Palace; and, moreover, unlike Huerta, Carranza, or possibly, even Villa, he would have had mass popular support at least in the south of the country and the capital. But, unlike the others, Zapata considered himself to be not a ruler of the people but their servant.

BY December 9, a large force of *Zapatistas* had arrived outside Puebla City. But they did not attack, as the supplies promised by Villa had not yet arrived. Zapata sent repeated requests to Villa, who was still encamped just outside Mexico City, for them. Day followed day, but they did not arrive. When at last Villa did let Zapata have them, the *Zapatistas* had to haul them by mule, or on their backs, through the pass of the great twin volcanoes of Ixaccihuatle and Popacateptl, because Villa refused to provide locomotives. But on December 15, the Liberation Army occupied Puebla without a fight. As soon as the *Carrancistas* and *Obregonistas* heard that Zapata had, at last, received the supplies, including some artillery, they took to their heels and fled.

On the day that Emiliano captured Puebla City, he was given the news that Villa had arrested and executed his secretary, Paulino Martinez. Zapata was disgusted. He was well aware of the strategic importance of holding Puebla; and he also wanted to destroy Carranza. Nevertheless, he and the Liberation Army returned to Morelos. There was, moreover, much constructive work to be done in the state. Emiliano practically retired as Supreme Chief of the Liberation Army of the South, and settled down in Tlaltizapan.

The short-lived 'coalition' between Villa and Zapata was at an end. All the *Zapatistas* had left both Puebla City and Puebla state by January 1st, 1915. Of the year to come, Gerrit Huizer comments:

'In 1915, a new government under Carranza tried to weaken and win to its cause the peasant revolutionary forces which practically controlled Mexico City. It published in Veracruz a Decree (January 6, 1915) which incorporated the main points of Zapata's programme, and which is generally considered to be the formal starting point of the Mexican land reform. This measure, together with the creation of battalions of urban workers which helped to combat the peasant armies, weakened peasant resistance. However, since no real effort was given to the new reform decree, the movement led by Zapata only withdrew from the capital, but retained military control in a large part of the states of Morelos, Guerrero and Puebla. In those areas a land distribution programme was carried out according to the rules of the *Plan de Ayala*, with the help of a group of students of the National School of Agriculture.'

IT was not a particularly happy Christmas for the inhabitants of Mexico City. There was a shortage of fuel. Food was scarce. Typhoid threatened to grow into an epidemic. And the paper money, now being printed in huge quantities by Villa, was worthless.

Furthermore Villa and his troops were administering typical *Villista* 'justice.' Within two weeks of his occupation, over one-hundred-and-fifty people had been executed by firing squads in the capital.

Gutierrez called upon the *Villistas* to stop taking the law into their own hands. Before the beginning of the year, however, Gutierrez had had enough. Finally, on January 16, he fled the capital and made his way home to San Luis Potosi. He had been interim president – in name at least – for just two months. Villa moved into a splendid mansion at 76 Calle Liverpool.

The Convention 'government' had not entirely disintegrated. It reassembled in Mexico City on New Year's Day, 1915. And on January 16, it elected the twenty-nine-year-old Roque Gonzalez Garza its presiding officer. By then, the Convention was largely *Zapatista*. But it was also largely a talking shop. Soto y Gama digressed over such people as Danton, Marat, Marx, Bakunin and Kropotkin. Nevertheless, Garza managed to bring some realism into the proceedings. A number of decisions were taken – but only by unanimous agreement. The Convention 'government' managed, to some extent, to 'police' the city; it also attempted to tackle the problem of the chaotic, and useless, currency in circulation. On January 23, it declared all Carranza money invalid.

A day or two previously, Villa's forces moved north. Villa also lost interest in the capital and, presumably, in the presidency as well. He left. Obregon, with a small but disciplined force of around 5,000 encamped at the archaeological site of San Juan Teotihuacan, just fifty kilometres from Mexico City, on January 25. The following day, most of the remaining *Zapatistas* evacuated the capital, and returned to Morelos, partly destroying the pumping station at Xochimilco, which was the city's principle source of water. The Convention rump transferred its headquarters to Cuernavaca, in Morelos.

On January 28, Obregon entered Mexico City, by then a dead city. Except for a few stray rifle shots from the Cathedral bell-tower in the Zocalo, there was no resistance. 'A few hundred *Zapatistas*,' writes Mrs. Moats, 'were left at the Palace . . . . running into the Palace, they barricaded the doors; and it was then that the *Carrancistas* discovered that Villa was on his way north.' Unlike after his previous entry into the capital, Obregon did not celebrate his 'victory.' He went straight to bed – with laryngitis.

By December 12, 1914, Carranza had published his land reform decree. And on January 6, 1915, his 'government' in Veracruz made it into a law. Despite its radical and reformist veneer, it was, in effect, entirely different from Zapata's *Plan de Ayala*. Its implementation was put in the hands of the state governors. Indeed, Carranza

116

expressly noted that his reform was 'not to revive the old communities, nor to create others like them'; he further stipulated that 'the property of the lands will not belong to the *pueblos* in common, but will be divided *inpleno domino*' – fee simple. Such was the *Carrancista* land reform law!

While Carranza tried to woo the *peones*, Obregon was doing likewise with the urban workers.

At the turn of the century, Ricardo Flores Magon, together with a number of his followers, established the *Casa del Obrero Mundial* (the House of the World Workers) in Mexico City. It was mainly a propagandist centre. But under the dictatorship of Don Porfirio Diaz it was soon closed down. It had, however, been reopened under Madero. In the main, the views propagated by the *Casa* were those of Kropotkin, Elisee Reclus and Malatesta. Antonio Diaz Soto y Gama had attended meetings organised by the *Casa*; but he had also been influenced by Leo Tolstoy.

Despite the *Casa's* precarious position, its influence was wider than was generally imagined. It also had links with the American Industrial Workers of the World, or 'Wobblies' as they were usually called. In August, 1914, Obregon contacted members of the *Casa del Obrero Mundial*. And in February, 1915, he negotiated with a number of prominent members of the *Casa*. The *Casa* then moved into a well-known colonial mansion known as the House of Tiles. Branches of the *Casa del Obrero Mundial* were established throughout areas controlled by Carranza and Obregon. In return, the *Casa* raised six 'Red Battalions' of workers to fight for Carranza against Villa. David Siqueiros, the young painter who later became a fanatical Communist and would-be NKVD assassin of Leon Trotsky, was a staff officer at Carranza's headquarters and also served as an advisor with the 'Red Battalions.'

Over the years, a few *Casa* members, such as Antonio Diaz Soto y Gama, had joined the *Zapatistas*, but most had not; and neither had many of the ordinary workers of Mexico City either. Now, the more 'progressive' workers of the *Casa del Obrero Mundial* were rallying to Carranza and Obregon. Robert Millon remarks:

'Carranza's programme of labour reform drew support from elements of the urban proletariat. These workers were attracted especially by the more radical elements within the Constitutionalist movement who presented themselves as *obreristas* (pro-labour) as well as *agraristas* (pro-peasant). They were not, however, attracted to the mainly rural *Zapatista insurrectos* of the south.'

117

Of course, Carranza and, probably to some extent, Obregon, knew what they were doing; but it is doubtful if many of the workers who formed and joined the 'Red Battalions', or many of the syndicalist members of the *Casa del Obrero Mundial*, did. Obregon convinced them that 'if they wanted to derive any benefit from the revolution, they could not remain outside it, but must participate.' So, they went off to fight the bandit-general, Pancho Villa. . . . .

CHAPTER XIII

MORELOS COMMUNE

BY the beginning of 1915, Morelos and much of the south of the country was peaceful. Almost immediately, the people began to elect their village chiefs and municipal representatives. A few of the chiefs had become tainted with the evils of militarism, but very few.

Emiliano Zapata, more than anyone, emphasised the importance of local, federalist, administration. Indeed, Zapata rebuked those chiefs who attempted to interfere in village affairs. Moreover, he never tried to organise or impose a centralised state police force in Morelos. Law enforcement, such as it was, remained the prerogative of the village councils. The result was local 'grassroots' democracy of a rough and ready kind. It also resulted, for the first time, in an administration whose objective was the restoration and development of the *ejidos*. At least the land question was being tackled in an orderly manner. To quite a considerable degree, the people of Morelos had to thank the meticulous, intense, twenty-nine-year-old Manuel Palafox for that. He was a ball of fire.

Within days of the Convention 'government' being set up in Mexico City, Palafox had been appointed Secretary of Agriculture. Early in January, he organised his department. He first founded a National Bank of Rural Loans; he also founded Regional Schools of Agriculture, and a National Factory of Agricultural Implements. And on January 14, he set up within the Department of Agriculture a Special Bureau of Land Division. He immediately began to review petitions for communal lands; and to villagers as far afield as Hidalgo and Guanajuato, he wrote suggesting that they reclaim their communal fields.

The administration of the agrarian programme began in Morelos as soon as technicians could be found to assist in carrying it out. Most of them were volunteers from the 1914 graduating class of the old

National School of Agriculture which, in 1913, had moved out of
Mexico City to the *Villista* headquarters in Chihuahua. But by 1914,
the School had decided to move south again. One of its leading
activists and principle teachers was Antonio Diaz Soto y Gama's
brother, Ignacio. By the end of January, ninety-five young agronomists had joined Palafox's agrarian commissions. They were charged
to survey and assist in the division of lands in Morelos, Guerrero,
Puebla and the Federal District.

On January 30, forty students and agronomists, carrying levels,
tripods and chains, arrived in Cuernavaca. Palafox also engaged a
number of military and civil engineers and technicians. They were
assigned to various parts of Morelos. Local *Zapatistas* found them old
mansions — formerly belonging to long-departed *hacendados* — for
their headquarters. Once a commission arrived in an area, the
agronomists, surveyors and technicians informed the local chiefs
when they were ready to start work, and the chiefs put up notices
informing the villagers.

Very many *pueblos* had already taken over the fields and other
lands from the *hacendados*. Nevertheless, the *peones* were prepared
to accept the offer of legalising their claims. First surveys were made.
A *pueblo* would quite often produce '*la mapa*' — the village land titles.
If there was no *mapa*, then a new claim would be made. After that,
the boundaries of the newly-acquired *ejidos* would be determined.
There were, of course, attempts by some villages to encroach upon
lands outside their areas, but not many. Usually, the villagers accepted
the commissioners' decisions. In a few instances, there were serious
conflicts. And in one or two cases, the villagers and commissioners
were forced to call upon General Zapata to decide the issue. But
the land surveys went ahead throughout Morelos and the neighbouring
states.

When a village had its boundaries surveyed, and had received its
alloted part of the *hacienda*, the commissioners left its administration
quite autonomous. According to article six of the land decree of
September 8, 1914, a *pueblo* could keep its land under a common
title, or it could distribute the titles among individual *rancheros,
peones* or *campesinos*. Both Palafox and Zapata had stressed that
custom and usage of each *pueblo* should determine the local system.
In each case it was for the people, in their assemblies, to decide.

'Thus,' notes John Womack, Jr., 'the villages were born anew. In
the months the six commissions functioned in the state they surveyed
and defined the boundaries of almost all the hundred-odd *pueblos*

120

there, incorporating into them most of the local farm land, stands of timber, and irrigation facilities.'

And by early March, 1915, Zapata was able to notify the Convention president, Roque Gonzalez Garza, that 'the matter relating to the agrarian question is resolved in a definitive manner, for the different *pueblos* of the state, in accord with the titles which protect their properties.' *Hacienda* lands not taken over by the villagers were not handed back to the planters, but were retained by the commissioners. The sugar-refining mills were also confiscated. Some were in ruins anyway. But both Palafox and Zapata wanted the mills back in operation, not as private, profit-making companies, but as common property of the people. Then, the villagers who produced cane could bring in their harvests.

BY early March, four of the state's mills were back in operation. Local *Zapatista* chiefs, such as Genovevo de la O, helped the workers run them. Morelos and its people began to prosper. In the Spring, harvesting began; the crops were not the planters' cane, or rice, but the traditional foodstuffs — corn and beans. And by mid-June reporters found all the fields in the state under cultivation.

Zapata, however, wanted more of the mills to open again. He ordered spare parts for damaged machines. And a little later, three more mills did open. Emiliano had opposed the 'plantation capitalism' of the *hacendados*, and their concentration on the production of sugar-cane to the exclusion of almost all other crops; but, once the planters and *hacendados* had gone, and the fields had been taken over again by the villagers, he urged them to diversify their crops.

'If you keep on growing chili peppers, onions and tomatoes,' he told them, 'you will never get out of the state of poverty you've always been in.'

So, he advised them to also grow cane as well.

'The agronomists and the Rural Land Bank will help you,' he added.

During the summer of 1915, for the first times in their lives, the people of Morelos began to eat well. After the terrors and vicissitudes of war, revolution and counter-revolution, Morelos had become almost a rural paradise . . . .

Emiliano made his headquarters, and his home, in the little town of Tlaltizapan, with its giant laurels and maze of canals leading down to the rice fields of Jojutla. Unlike in Mexico City under Huerta, Villa or Obregon, there was no display of confiscated luxury, no consumption of captured treasure, no swarm of bureaucrats jumping from telephone to limosine. Emiliano Zapata spent most of his days in an office, in an old rice mill, dealing with land claims, and corresponding with Palafox. In the evenings, he and his companions relaxed in the *plaza*, drinking, smoking cigars, and discussing horses and the like. And at night, Emiliano slept with one or other of his two or three regular women friends — he fathered at least two children during his stay in Tlaltizapan. On his birthday in August, the people held a *fiesta* with a parade, songs, poetry-reading, children's games and, later, a bullfight.

But war clouds were, yet again, beginning to drift towards Morelos .

OBREGON occupied Mexico City — for six weeks. He did not intend to stay long anyway. Nevertheless, he more than made his presence felt while there. Many houses and churches were sacked by his troops. Factory equipment was dismantled and sent to Veracruz. Furniture was removed from government offices. Cars and horses were confiscated. Schools were closed down. Many of the people were starving.

On February 3, all *Villista* currency was declared worthless; and it was, for the second time, replaced by *Carrancista* money. The banks were then shut down. Merchants were forced at gunpoint to open their safes. Those suspected of hoarding money or food were made to sweep the streets. Obregon reminded the Church that it had donated forty million pesos to Huerta; and ordered the clergy to raise five hundred million pesos 'for relief of the city poor.' When the priests refused to pay up, he had one-hundred-and-eight of them drafted into the *Carrancista* army, of whom over fifty were found to be suffering from VD.

On March 10, Obregon left the capital in preparation for his showdown with Villa.

With Obregon in occupation of Mexico City, the *Zapatistas* had successfully stopped all food and other supplies from getting through. But as he moved out, units of the Liberation Army of the South moved in. The population was relieved; and even a few church bells began to ring. And with the return of the *Zapatistas*, the water supply, which they had cut off, was restored. The Convention 'government,' by then almost entirely *Zapatista* in outlook, also decided to return to the capital. Villa wired Zapata, warning him that the Convention would find itself forced to flee again. He offered to accommodate it at his headquarters in Chihuahua, together with his own Convention 'government.' But on March 21, the Convention did reconvene in Mexico City, under its provisional president, Roque Gonzalez Garza.

The Convention tried to draft a programme to serve as a social and political charter for the revolution. But progress was constantly interrupted by the growing friction between the *Zapatista* majority and the small, but vociferous, *Villista* minority. The *Villistas* were not really interested in the land question; but they had become particularly critical of Zapata for not marching on Veracruz. The *Zapatistas*, on the other hand, complained that Villa had never kept his word over the delivery of war supplies. What he had sent had been too little and too late, they said. Furthermore, the Convention president, Roque Gonzalez Garza, was extremely hostile towards Manuel Palafox, whom, he claimed, was using too many supplies, and too much manpower, on his agricultural programme in Morelos and the south. Garza finally had a showdown with Zapata, who was in a belligerent mood. Garza and a companion agreed to ride out of Mexico City and meet Zapata at a halfway point. When they met, Emiliano threatened Garza with his revolver, but Garza stood his ground, insisting that he was president of the Convention, and that his authority was superior to the Supreme Chief of the Liberation Army of the South and Centre. The two men, however, calmed down; and Zapata agreed to ride with Garza into the capital for further talks at the National Palace. Discussion was brief, and there was no agreement. 'Zapata,' remarks William Weber Johnson, 'rode his horse on to the platform car of the city tramlines, which delivered him to Xochimilco. From there he rode over the mountains to Morelos, and never again came back to the city.'

On June 9, 1915, Roque Gonzalez Garza, who had offered to resign as provisional president, was voted out of office by the *Zapatista* majority in the Convention, and was replaced by his secretary, Francisco Lagos Chazaro, who said that he would work for the unity of the *Zapatistas* and the *Villistas* — a forlorn hope indeed. Garza left Mexico City to fight for Villa against the Constitutionalist forces of Carranza and Obregon. And in July, the Convention finally dissolved. The delegates dispersed. The *Zapatistas* returned to Cuernavaca; the others moved to Toluca, where some of them continued to call themselves the Convention government.

In Mexico City the food situation had become desperate. And on July 11, the *Carrancista* general, Pablo Gonzalez, entered the capital, only to evacuate it again six days later. A few remaining *Zapatistas*

Alvaro Obregon

Manuel Palafox

Antonio Diaz Soto y Gama

had already fled back to Morelos. By August 2, General Gonzalez reoccupied the city. The capital had changed hands for the last time . . . .

Emiliano Zapata and the Morelos chiefs began at last to concern themselves with the changing military situation. The agronomists and technicians — whose work was largely completed — found that they were unable to return to Mexico City. Zapata finally went into action. At the end of July, he attacked a small force of about 1,500 *Carrancistas* northeast of Mexico City, with a force of more than 7,000 *Zapatistas*. Agents had reported to Zapata that they were intending to invade Morelos. Attack was, as always, the best form of defence. Zapata then launched a number of attacks simultaneously against the *Carrancistas* in Puebla, Mexico State and the Federal District. And in September, he captured the electric power station at Necaxa, which supplied the capital with its electricity, but he could not hold it against *Carrancista* attacks. The *Carrancistas* (now part of the newly-formed Constitutionalist Army under the command of Alvaro Obregon) soon pushed the *Zapatistas* out of the Valley of Mexico.

War clouds were now very close indeed. Morelos was, once again, in danger.

OBREGON and his highly disciplined Constitutionalist Army, which also included divisions of the old Federal Army, moved north during March, 1915, to Cazadero, in Queretaro. There, they waited for supplies and reinforcements from Carranza in Veracruz. Obregon then moved towards Celaya, the site he had chosen for his showdown with Villa.

Angeles, some three days away, was racing to Villa's support by forced marches. He advised Villa to wait. But Villa, reckless and impatient as ever, would not listen to wiser and cooler councils. He had at his base at Aguascalientes, about 15,000 men; and on April 6, he moved south to Irapuato, within striking distance of Obregon's forces. Villa then advanced in three columns upon Celaya without reconnaissance, and less than two hundred rounds of ammunition to a man. After a brief shelling of enemy positions, Villa threw his entire massed cavalry against Obregon's entrenchments. It was a massacre. By dusk, Villa had left over 1,000 men dead on the field; and his hospital trains were overwhelmed with wounded. Many of the horses had been torn to pieces on the barbed wire.

Yet next morning, Villa redoubled his efforts. His artillery at first pounded Obregon's front-line troops. Then, Villa, leading his

dorados in person, threw his cavalry against Obregon's trenches.
Again, it was a massacre. The battle lasted all day. The *Villistas*
were driven back, leaving more than 3,000 dead and wounded.

Villa withdrew his exhausted and depleted army northwards to
Hacienda de Trojes. There, he at least received Angeles' reinforcements.
He now had an army of more than 30,000 men, including 14,000
cavalry and thirty-six pieces of artillery. Yet again he could not
wait. At dawn on April 13, Villa's army returned to the assault. As
before, Villa led his cavalry against trenches rendered almost
invulnerable by an interlacing breastwork of barbed wire. Attack
followed attack. And by sundown, the most powerful army Villa
had ever commanded was retreating in wild disorder.

Pancho managed to escape by train to the north. He admitted
that he had lost over 6,000 men. Falling back on Trinidad, in
Guanajuato, Villa endeavoured to reorganise his forces. But he was
now critically short of ammunition. During the rest of the summer
of 1915, he fought a number of engagements with the *Carrancistas*,
but each ended in defeat and humiliation. He retreated all the way
to Ciudad Juarez opposite El Paso on the Texas border. In November
he fought his last battle – and lost it. His army was virtually wiped
out, reduced to less than 1,400 men – half-starved and ammunitionless.
Mexico's bloodiest episode had come to an end.

After a while, Doroteo Arango, alias Pancho Villa, returned to
banditry and cattle rustling. Meanwhile, in the south, Emiliano
Zapata also had his back to the wall.

CHAPTER XIV

BACK AGAINST THE WALL

VENUSTIANO Carranza, the Spanish aristocrat, came to power with
the blessing of the White House; and, like Don Porfirio Diaz before
him, he proceeded with ruthlessness and vigour to establish 'order'
in the country.

He was soon able, with the assistance and military genius of Alvaro
Obregon, to tighten his grip on large areas of Mexico. He was also
able to deploy an increasing number of his troops against the enemy
in the south – Emiliano Zapata and his Indian *peone* 'horde.' Before
he could boast that he was master of Mexico, Carranza would have
to wipe out not only the Liberation Army of the South, but
Zapatismo itself. And he was certain that that would be a shorter,

easier, and less bloody, struggle than Obregon's campaigns against Villa. Furthermore, Carranza could now obtain arms and ammunition from America. On the other hand, he knew that the *Zapatistas* were not all that well off for ammunition and other supplies.

While Zapata was resting in Tlaltizapan, and most of the Liberation Army were engaged in work on their newly-won lands, Carranza appointed General Pablo Gonzalez — who, it had been said, had never won a battle — as military commander in Morelos and the south. As a former chief of the secret police, he was more than determined to 'win his spurs' by annihilating Zapata. His orders were to destroy Morelos from the Ajuscos to the Rio Amecusac.

BUT first of all, Don Venustiano tried the old trick: he offered Emiliano a *hacienda* and 100,000 pesos if he would give up the struggle. Zapata was not for sale. He was more than willing to discuss demobilisation provided Carranza officially accepted and endorsed the principles of the *Plan de Ayala*. But the old *hacendado* would not listen.

Nevertheless, in August, 1915, he declared an amnesty. A few prominent *Zapatistas* accepted. This gave rise to tensions among some of the chiefs within the *Zapatista* camp. Most of the chiefs, however, remained loyal to Zapata and the cause for which they had fought and struggled for so long. Others merely did neither one thing or the other. As in the past, they just waited to see what would happen.

Of all the Morelos chiefs, Genovevo de la O, who, in the past, had been the most independent, proved to be most loyal, and the most active. He attempted to control all the telegraph offices in his area north of Cuernavaca. And after *Carrancistas*, sweeping up from Acapulco on the Pacific Coast, had taken Chilpancingo and Iguala, and had entered Morelos, Genovevo de la O and his *insurrectos* drove them all the way back to the coast in a terrific counter-offensive. Indeed, his forces almost captured Acapulco itself. Other chiefs began to take up the challenge. Sometimes in the face of as many as three of four separate *Carrancista* columns advancing into the state, they would employ the tactics of ambush.

A hundred or more scattered detachments of the Liberation Army, under the general command of Zapata, strove to hold back the Constitutionalist invaders. All Morelos, to the last man, woman and *muchacho*, was in the fight. Resistance also began over a large part of Puebla to the west, of Guerrero to the south, of Oaxaca to the southwest and of the State of Mexico to the east. Zapata's supplies of ammunition dwindled. And on February 1, 1916, about 20,000 *Carrancista* troops joined the 10,000 already assigned to the south. Carranza also threatened to use the government's recently acquired fleet of aircraft to bomb *Zapatista* camps, and give them 'a mortal blow.'

Throughout March, General Pablo Gonzalez attacked *Zapatista*-controlled towns and strongholds. Huitzilac was given up without a fight, with the *Zapatistas* retreating south to Cuentepec. Carranza's forces immediately — and without resistance — drove on to La Cruz, a little over ten kilometres from the Morelos state capital of Cuernavaca. Gonzalez controlled the heights around the city. De la O harassed, and held up, the *Carrancistas* for a while.

Emiliano Zapata had to continually withdraw, and concentrate his forces closer to the Rio Amecusac.

Volunteer Tarahumara Indians from Durango and Tarascan warriors from Michoacan arrived in Morelos; but Gonzalez was able to ring the entire state with his 30,000 men. Once again, Zapata and the Liberation Army of the South were in conflict with the Mexican state and government. Once again, Zapata was, in the words of Harry Dunn, 'the greatest outlaw in the Western World.'

On May 2, Gonzalez began his attack on Cuernavaca. Emiliano arrived soon after with a small detachment of his 'Death Legion.' But he was too late. And his forces were too small. After using one of their new aircraft to bomb *Zapatista* entrenchments, the Constitutionalists swept into Cuernavaca. Zapata and his small force of horsemen escaped just in time. They rode as fast as they could back to their base at Tlaltizapan. A few days later, both Cuautla and Yautepec fell to General Gonzalez. Then Villa de Ayala was overrun.

Zapata remarked to a comrade: 'More than 30,000 Federals are going towards Tlaltizapan.'

'This is our last stronghold . . . . We will defend it,' replied his comrade.

But Emiliano found himself increasingly isolated in his mountain redoubt. And worse was to come. Zapata's 'mountain redoubt' was finally overrun. At Tlaltizapan, Pablo Gonzalez captured a considerable amount of booty. He also executed almost three hundred people, of whom over half were women and children — relatives and friends of the *Zapatistas* headquarters' staff.

Gonzalez began a wave of terror in Morelos. By mid-May, 1916, about 1,500 *Zapatista* prisoners of war had been sent to the dreaded concentration camps of Yucatan, just as had thousands of unfortunate *peones* and workers during Don Porfirio's dictatorship. But Gonzalez was only following Carranza's orders. Edcumb Pinchon comments: 'he (Carranza) prosecutes against Zapata a brutal campaign of extermination, laying waste whole sections of the country with as little mercy upon non-combatants, women and children, as Diaz ever had shown.'

Carranza's policy of scorched earth was working with ferocious efficiency, with the countryside swarming with refugees. Zapata and his staff had to organise some kind of rescue, and refuge, for the victims of Carranza's terror. It was no easy task. Already much of the northern third of Morelos had been laid waste. Emiliano and the chiefs decided that, where possible, all the older men and women, and young children, would have to move to the safety of the mountains encircling the Valley of Morelos. Pichon vividly describes what happened.

'So began a tragic hegira . . . .

Desperately loading their goods and remaining stores of food into carts yoked to their cows, or upon *burros* burdened till they crumpled to the earth or swinging upon their shoulders such packs as made the mountain trails appear crawling with huge snails, the folk of half a hundred villages, shepherded by posses of heavily armed *charros*, bid *adios* to their *tierra chica*, and set their faces toward they knew not what.

Zapata's plan was to move the folk to the mountains nearest them, not only because they would have more chance to survive in a country well known to them, but because he knew they would refuse to go where, if they should die, they might not be carried at midnight down to the ancestral graveyard. And so, to the far north the ancient, undefeated *pueblo* of deep Tepoztlan became an empty place. The folk had fled to the vast clefts and ravines in the crest of the Sierra Ajusco. The villagers of the west retreated to the apocalyptic gorges of the Sierra Chalma, the villagers of the east to the tossed-up chaos of the Sierra Puebla. While the valleys remained the main theatre of war, the mountains became the haunt of a gypsy army, living in the thousand merciful caves that pocketed the frequent limestone formations.

The mountains offered a plentiful supply of wood and water. These were everywhere. But food was another matter. Game was scarce. And what there was quickly was driven away by the presence of this moving horde. And, with every able-bodied marksman needed on the fighting line, the only available hunters were men too old and slow for war.

Quickly realising that he had saved these folk from massacre only to deliver them over to slow starvation, Zapata struggled to organise a line of food supplies. Picked forces, usually held in reserve for critical military action, were organised into raiding parties. The largest of these he led himself. In modern parlance they would be dubbed 'suicide squads.' Their business was to worm through the enemy's lines, capture his pack-mule commissary trains and lead them off into the mountains. Few of the raiding parties long survived; but while they lived they raided, and while they raided, thousands of old women and stricken, starving children were fed.

At the same time behind the lines, Zapata insisted that every inch of earth be tilled. The moment fighting relaxed, the rifle was dropped for the hoe. Zapata himself, setting the example, full of courage and encouragement, stripped to the waist and worked with his men. No sooner had one detachment been organised for the tasks of production than he was off to another point on the line and plunging in, himself always the first with plough or hoe.'

Zapata was not, however, alone, though he was the moving and organising spirit of the struggle against Carranza.

IN 1914, Mrs. Rosa E. King, the English woman who had owned a teashop and, later, the Bella Vista Hotel in Cuernavaca, abandoned her properties during a *Zapatista* attack on the city and, with the remnants of the Federal garrison, fled. Later, she heard that, during the fighting, the hotel had been destroyed or, at least, partially damaged. In 1916, she decided, against the advice of the British Consul in Veracruz, to return to Cuernavaca. Rosa King describes her experiences and what she found there.

'Late in the afternoon the train reached Cuernavaca. What a sight to greet us! Black, battered, bullet-pierced walls where there had been comfortable, happy homes; bridges destroyed, approaches to the town cut off; everywhere signs of the dreaded conflict that had taken place .... My head had known that it would be like this, but my heart was not prepared. We drove down the silent streets past abandoned, deserted houses; not a soul in sight. A dog, nosing in a heap of rubbish, slunk away at our approach, and the clatter of the wheels awoke strange echoes of emptiness. In the heart of the town a handful of people were living, and I saw the soldiers, their uniforms marking them as strangers. Some of my servants had clung to the

Bella Vista, and I found them waiting for me in the ruin of the portal.'

Later, Mrs. King met General Pablo Gonzalez.

'He had his own obsesssion, the crushing of his elusive foe in any way he could compass it, and my obsession (of repairing the hotel) wearied him. I remember the moment when his patience snapped.

"This is no time to talk of reconstruction, *Senora* King! Will you not comprehend, *senora* – I am about to destroy what still remains of Cuernavaca!" He went on talking, saying that there was no stamping out of Zapata because all the towns and villages roundabout sheltered *Zapatistas* in their need; so that he was going to sack them all, including Cuernavaca, and thus run his fox into the open. I scarcely heard him.

"But our homes! Our property!" I cried.

"Oh, *senora*!", he said almost angrily. "That is of the past. That is all over . . . ."

I walked back to the heart of the town like one coming out of a daze.'

Rosa King climbed the hill by Corte's Palace . . . .

'I looked across the wasted valley, to the unchanged beauty of its slopes and the encircling ranks of its protecting mountain ranges. They were strong, steadfast, eternal – but so far away. Rebelliously, I called to them, "Are you dead, too?" Then voices across the valley; voices of Toltecs and Chichemecans from their homes of centuries ago at the feet of the white volcanoes; voices of Tlahuicas from their ancient citadel, Cuauhnahuac, where they battled to hold their freedom and their country; voices saying, "The very ruins all about you are telling you we live. Free-born men, like the mountains, will always survive." And the motionless foothills seemed to surge with the shadows of the men I knew lay hiding there, with their rifles and their leader, finding cover and nourishing herbs among the stoney ledges.'

Mrs. King, the teashop lady from England, understood the *Zapatistas* far better than had Don Porfirio or Don Francisco Madero, or General Huerta, or Don Venustiano Carranza or even the tempestuous bandit-rebel, Pancho Villa. And General Gonzalez, who was systematically ravaging the beautiful Valley of Morelos, did not fully understand either; though he did at least realise that, in their hearts, all the ordinary men and women of Morelos were *Zapatistas*, and that by only wiping out every town and *pueblo* could he hope to destroy *Zapatismo*.

131

'Free-born men, like the mountains, will always survive' . . . . And they did! They just went on fighting – they were a people in arms.

General Pablo Gonzalez ruled – or, at least, tried to rule – Morelos and the south just like a military dictator. He also looted on a grand scale. He 'shipped out furniture and other movables by car-loads after destroying the *haciendas* by fire' writes Mrs. Moats. 'He scraped off every inch of copper and steel, and sold everything for his own account.' Almost all the iron in Morelos was removed and sold as acrap to the Europeans who required it for their own war. Gonzalez also removed herds of cattle grazing in the rich pasture lands, particularly around Tlaltizapan, as well as the recent cane harvest, milling machines from the factories – and even Zapata's own little printing press, which he had captured.

Parkes comments:

'Gonzalez lived up to his reputation. What he lacked in general-ship was compensated in plunder and destruction. He alleged that Zapata was to be starved into submission, and his army, which deserved better than that of Zapata to be called an army of bandits, completed the ruin of Morelos.'

Under such conditions and circumstances, Zapata and the chiefs were forced to disband the Liberation Army as a large united force. It had never really been a fully-centralised, positional army in the generally-accepted sense of the word anyway.

And now the *Zapatistas* had neither enough ammunition or food supplies for a regular positional army. They, therefore, reverted, as they had always done in times of trouble, to being a loose federation of *guerrilleros*, comprising scores of scattered groups of twenty to one hundred men and women. They based themselves in temporary camps and hideouts in the hills and mountains; and throughout July, 1916, they made swift sorties against the *Carrancista* forces of occupation.

One group of *guerrilleros* struck deep into the Federal District, where it captured a considerable amount of military supplies, and then withdrew. At the end of July, Zapata attacked the garrison holding his old headquarters at Tlaltizapan. In August, the *Zapatistas* probably numbered around 6,000, with about 2,000 in reserve. Gonzalez still had 30,000 men in the state. A few Morelos chiefs had come to terms with the government; these Zapata condemned as traitors. Most of the chiefs who continued the struggle had been with Emiliano from the start.

General Gonzalez continued to destroy hamlets and *pueblos*, and

132

General Pablo Gonzalez

Gildardo Magana

to shoot batches of villagers. *Zapatista guerrilleros* raided supply dumps for arms and ammunition. And they went on fighting. They ambushed careless government troops; and they began to blow up trains again. They cut communications. The tide began to turn.

Throughout the states of Guerrero, Hidalgo, Mexico State, Oaxaca and Puebla, local and often independent *Zapatistas* harassed Carranza's columns. On November 11, General Pablo Gonzalez, now at his wits' end, ordered that anyone found helping the *Zapatistas* would be shot on sight. Troop-train after troop-train was dynamited. And, as the days went by, explosions could be heard nearer and nearer to the heart of Mexico City itself. With his 30,000 men, Gonzalez was helpless; and by the end of the year, weakened by malaria and frustrated by uncertainty, his army was finally withdrawn from Morelos. And by the end of January, 1917, the *Zapatistas* had reoccupied Cuautla, Jonacatepec, Yautepec and even Cuernavaca. Shortly after Emiliano Zapata returned to his headquarters at Tlaltizapan. The people of Morelos, as well as those of Guerrero and Puebla, had repelled their enemies. They had, it is true, retrieved no supplies, but they had recovered their states.

Unfortunately, however, Morelos and the south was in a very bad way. Families had been uprooted; towns and *pueblos* had been destroyed; cattle, pigs and poultry had been killed off, or had been stolen by the *Carrancistas*, and the *haciendas* were no more. Most of the *pueblos* were incapable of supporting their people, or of running their own affairs.

Emiliano Zapata was particularly concerned over the disintegration and disorganisation of the *pueblos*, and of town and city administration generally. He was also beginning to concern himself with the effectiveness of the reconstituted Liberation Army of the South and Centre. On the other hand, the *Zapatistas* had been successfully intensifying their propaganda war against Carranza and the government over the last twelve months or so – and were to continue to do so for some time.

CHAPTER XV

WAR OF WORDS

IN Novermber, 1916, Zapata urged Antonio Diaz Soto y Gama and other *Zapatista* secretaries to visit the *pueblos* and explain that

Zapatismo 'rose up in arms,' not to protect the bandits or banditry, or self-seeking chiefs, but to guarantee the rights of the *pueblos*, and take back the *ejidos* and common lands which the *hacendados* had stolen from them.

On November 28, Soto y Gama, Palafox, Montano, the Magana brothers, and about ten others organised, at Zapata's office in Tlaltizapan, the 'Consultation Centre For Revolutionary Propaganda and Unification.' The aim of the centre was to assist the *pueblos* by giving talks on such topics as mutual obligations of the armed *Zapatistas*, explanations of manifestos, decrees and circulars, which were being issued from the headquarters; and members of the centre were also asked to mediate in feuds between individual chiefs, *pueblos* and, even more important, help organise juntas in all villages as 'Associations for the Defence of Revolutionary Principles.' They did not however, attempt − or even wish − to organise a political party.*

At the end of 1916 and the beginning of 1917, therefore, many associations were formed in Morelos, Puebla and elsewhere. In many cases, they were the first ever popular organisations of a non-military, civilian nature to have existed in some villages. They had no official authority; but they soon dominated local society. All association representatives had to be elected by direct vote every four months by all the members of their respective *pueblos*. Each representative had to reside in the *pueblo* Re-election for a year after leaving office was strictly forbidden. And serving members of the Liberation Army were not allowed to stand for election. The representatives' functions were varied. They helped to organise local municipal elections, ensured civil control over the Liberation Army, mediated in occasional disputes between municipal officials, as well as between village chiefs and Liberation Army commanders. They also mediated in conflicts relating to local resources − water, crops, pastures, draft animals. And they furthered *Zapatista* propaganda and decrees.

By early 1917, a rudimentary *Zapatista* administration began to take shape in Morelos and elsewhere in the south. Emiliano, particularly, realised that *pueblos* isolated from each other often fell

*Gerrit Huizer, in his PEASANT REBELLION IN LATIN AMERICA, states that"In Mexico there was initially no united and organised group or party with a more or less specific purpose or ideology behind the revolution.' (p.64).

This is not, however, quite true: the MAGONISTA group was small, but it was organised and it had a 'specific purpose'. See LAND AND LIBERTY by Ricardo Flores Magon, edited by David Poole.

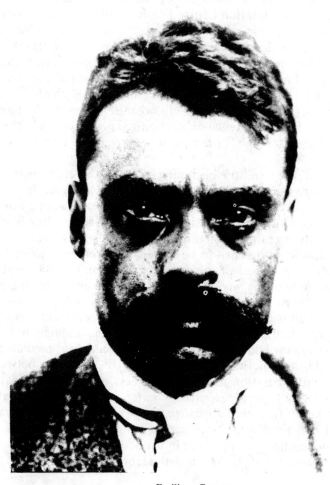

Emiliano Zapata

into decay and rivalry; so, he and the secretaries instituted a new office to serve as a bond between *municipos* — that of a district president. Tentative arrangements were made to hold elections for a new state governor, but hostilities began late in the summer of 1917, and the arrangements came to nothing.

DURING 1916 and 1917, Zapata was concerned over the effectiveness of the Liberation Army of the South. He attempted to organise the various groups efficiently. His aim was to reorganise the army on the basis of infantry, cavalry and artillery units, with supporting engineering, sanitation and other administrative services. But, in spite of Zapata's efforts, the Liberation Army never attained the 'discipline' and organisation of a regular army.

Nevertheless, Robert P. Millon (an admirer of the Vietcong) is forced to admit that, 'In spite of their shortcomings in organisation, Zapata's men were quite effective fighters. They laid traps and ambushes, cut supply lines, took small towns by storm, destroyed the smaller enemy units and harassed his larger ones. They were expert at capturing the elements of war from the enemy and, in addition, fabricated explosives and cartridges on their own. True to the tenets of guerrilla warfare, they avoided formal battles with major enemy forces until they were fairly certain of victory, thereby denying the enemy the opportunity to destroy them as an effective military force at one blow (as Obregon did the *Villistas*).'

Octavio Paz has also given a vivid account of the effectiveness of *Zapatista* tactics against Pablo Gonzalez's *Carrancista* forces in 1916 and the beginning of 1917, when they were forced to withdraw from Morelos and the South. According to Paz, Zapata maintained only a small force at his headquarters which, in an emergency, could be speedily sent into action at almost any place, and at almost any time. Moreover, the various individual guerrilla units were constantly on the move, attacking the *Carrancistas* in not only Morelos, but the states of Mexico, Hidalgo, Oaxaca, Puebla and Tlazcala as well.

'These tactics,' says Paz, 'completely disconcerted the enemy who could never put his fire power into effective use. If the enemy advanced with a large force, he never found anyone to fight; if he divided his forces, he exposed them to destruction in ambushes and assaults.'

One prominent *Carrancista*, Luis Cabrera, speaking in the National Congress in 1917, recognised the effectiveness of Zapata's methods, when he claimed that though it was easy to defeat the *Zapatistas* economically, it was indeed quite difficult to conquer them militarily.

And in 1917, Carranza appointed yet another new general, Cesareo Castro, to finish off the *Zapatistas*. By the end of the year, Zapata was quite hard pressed. Nevertheless, Castro achieved very little success; so Pablo Gonzalez was recalled. He managed to capture Cuautla, Jonatepec and Zacualpan. However, as in the past, the campaign against Zapata soon fizzled out. The Liberation Army was unable to retake Cuautla, but managed to hang on to Yautepec, Tlaltizapan and a number of other towns. There was something of a stalemate.

Emiliano was far from happy.

Earlier in the year, he had suffered a number of personal losses. An old comrade, Lucino Cabrera, who had helped him defend Anenecuilco seven years ago, deserted Zapata, and became a crooked dealer in scrap metal. Then, Emiliano's brother, Eufemio started to drink far too much. He beat up an old man, and was shot and killed in a street battle on June 18, by Sidronio Camacho who, with a small group of *Zapatistas*, went north and accepted a Carranza amnesty. Emiliano Zapata's old school-teacher friend and collaborator of the *Plan de Ayala*, Otilio Montano, had a number of disagreements with some of Zapata's headquarters' staff at Tlaltizapan, and retired to the town of Buenavista de Cuellar, on the Guerrero border. But in May, 1917, an anti-*Zapatista* rebellion broke out in the town. The rebels demanded recognition of Carranza. The alleged leader was hanged; but a number of captured rebels claimed that Montano was the brains behind the revolt. He vigorously denied the charge, but there seemed to be some evidence against him. Palafox and Soto y Gama were convinced that he was guilty. And on May 18, a 'Revolutionary Tribunal' found him guilty. Zapata was, however, far from convinced. But at noon the next day, Montano was executed by firing squad.

Emiliano had lost two old comrades and his brother. The future did not look bright . . . .

FROM 1915 onwards, the *Zapatistas* issued a spate of manifestos, expositions, circulars and military directives. Some were directly from Zapata; but most emanated from the headquarters' secretaries, or from the Convention 'remnants' in Cuernavaca.

The Convention, under *Zapatista* influence, issued an Agrarian Law, on October 26, 1915, which provided for the implementation of the *Plan de Ayala*. And on the same day, Palafox and Soto y Gama published their *Manifesto to the Nation*, calling for various reforms on such diverse subjects as the *ejidos*,education, taxes — and even divorce! On April 18, 1916, the Convention issued a 'Regulatory Law on the National Agrarian Question,' as well as a 'Programme of Politico-Social Reforms.' These declared that 'the supreme end of the revolution is the division of the lands among the peasants'; and that 'the *peones* right away, and by force of arms, should and can recover the properties which were taken from them in the epoch of the dictatorship.'

And the Convention 'law' said that those villages who had not yet done so in accordance with the *Plan de Ayala* should immediately take possession of the lands.

At the end of May, 1916, Zapata issued a circular authorising villagers to organise and arm themselves in defence against 'evildoers and bad revolutionaries.' In June, he sent out circulars to chiefs warning them against moves by Felix Diaz to obtain their support in his struggle against Carranza. And on September 15, the secretaries decreed a 'General Law on Municipal Liberties.' Its objective was to abolish the system of political prefectures, and Federal, state, control over local town councils. Three days later, they published a 'law' on 'State and Municipal Incomes for the State of Morelos.'

The *Zapatista* propaganda war continued unabated.

On October 1, 1916, Zapata circulated his *Exposition to the Mexican People*. In it he denounced Carranza as a despot who had deceived the people with false revolutionary promises. Carranza, he claimed, had returned the *haciendas* to the planters, had broken workers' strikes and had, among other things, restricted freedom.

Zapata, unlike Carranza and Obregon, expressed his belief in freedom of religious conscience, arguing that the *Carrancista* attacks on churches and their crude anti-religious propaganda was, in fact, demogogic and counter-revolutionary. It was, he said, diversionary, and done to conceal the *Carrancistas'* lack of revolutionary content in their economic and social programmes. Emiliano Zapata — who was not himself religious — declared that 'these attacks upon religious cults and popular conscience are counter-productive and prejudicial because they persuade no one, convince no one; they only exacerbate passions, create martyrs, awaken more vividly the superstitions which they wish to dominate, and give strength to the enemy whom they pretend to fight.' Zapata ended by stressing that the revolution was the taking back of the land by the *peones* from those who had stolen it, and liberty and justice for all the people.

After seven years of struggle, Zapata's cry was still *'tierra y libertad!'*

— the phrase originally popularised by Ricardo Flores Magon in his paper, *Regeneracion.*

Also in October, 1916, Zapata sent out 'Instructions to Chiefs of Detachments' to 'shoot on the spot any person caught in the act of banditry or abuse of local rights.' Banditry, though not endemic in Morelos, had become something of a problem, as elsewhere in Mexico, after so many years of civil strife.

On January 20, 1917, Zapata issued another *Manifesto to the Mexican People*, in which he again stated the objectives of the *Zapatistas* in similar broad terms to that of the previous manifesto of October 1, 1917. He referred to 'the nightmare of *Carrancismo*, running over with horror and blood.' And again he said that the revolution sought to distribute the land free to the *peones*. Carranza, on the other hand, merely offered destruction, despoilation, autocracy and the continued domination of Mexico by the *hacendados*, and the *caciques*. On April 20, Zapata published yet another *Manifesto to the People*, in much the same vein as the two previous ones. But the latter was a very personal attack upon the 'First Chief,' Carranza.

Circulars, decrees and manifestos continued to pour forth from the *Zapatista* headquarters during 1917.

In a circular published on April 17, it was noted that many villagers had established primary schools, as well as a few night schools, in Morelos and a number of other states, and that a 'manual arts' school was soon to open in Tochimizolco. On May 1, Zapata issued a *Protest Before the Mexican People,* in which he criticised Carranza for attempting to curry favour with the government of the United States. And in August, Zapata again set out his views on education. In a circular dated August 22, he declared:

'Now, you know perfectly well that one of the ideals for which we are fighting is that of fomenting public education, and if under the pretext that the times through which we are passing are abnormal we were to neglect such important a branch we would contravene our own ideals, which should not happen for any reason.'

On September 1, another *Manifesto to the Nation* was issued from Zapata's headquarters. It claimed that Carranza was a bogus revolutionary, and that the Republic's 'true revolutionaries' were still fighting for the implementation of the *Plan de Ayala.*

After October, 1917, the propaganda war against the Carranza government largely ceased. Militarily, the *Zapatistas* were again on the defensive, and had little time for publishing and propagandising.

Furthermore, 'diplomatic' overtures were being made by the government to the *Zapatistas*, as well as similar ones, by some *Zapatistas*, to various factions in the capital and the north, including the *Villista* remnants. At the same time, Emiliano Zapata was becoming increasingly depressed and taciturn. Often, he would sit alone, reading history books.

CHAPTER XVI

CARRANZA CONSOLIDATES

DURING 1915, the *Carrancistas*, partly under the 'left' influence of Alvaro Obregon and partly for tactical reasons, attempted to placate the peasants and the workers. Obregon formed his alliance with the *Casa del Obrero Mundial* in Mexico City and, in return, received considerable assistance in his campaign against Villa from units of the workers' 'Red Battalions', whilst Carranza wooed the *peones* with his agricultural and land proposals.

In the state of Yucatan, the pro-*Carrancista* general and state governor, Salador Alvarado, actually took Carranza's proposals seriously. He attacked and looted the churches. But he also used state funds to form workers' *Ligas de Resistencia* – pressure groups. Yucatan's almost exclusive source of income was *henequen*. Alvarado, therefore, created a *Commission Reguladora del Mercado de Henequen*, a body for planning and commercialising its cultivation. He organised *henequen ejidos* into cooperatives to process the crop, and set up departments to promote its development. He took over the local railroads, and a number of public works. He issued a decree that there should be a school in every *ejido*, and loans were offered for their construction. He also promulgated an agrarian law which affirmed that 'no one is the exclusive owner of land, any more than light and air.' Such policies almost verged upon *Zapatismo*! There were so many protests from the well-to-do elements within the state that Carranza annuled the legislation.

In October, 1915, Carranza felt sufficiently confident of his position in the country to leave his base in Veracruz; but he avoided Mexico City, as it was, he admitted, still too vulnerable to attack by the *Zapatistas*. So he went to Tampico, where he greeted Obregon. On December 29, he boarded the presidential train. And on the last day of the year, he arrived in the old colonial city of Queretaro, which, he asserted, would become both his residence and the new capital of Mexico.

By the end of 1915, Carranza had established control over much of Mexico. Only Zapata continued to resist him. On April 14, 1916, Carranza suddenly returned to Mexico City. He had changed his mind. It was now to be his capital.

Mexico, however, was far from being a happy and tranquil country. Parkes describes the situation thus:

'One ruling class had been overthrown by another. In the place of the Diaz governors and the *jefes politicos*, who might be tyrannical and grafting but who at least had been under the control of the dictatorship, there had arisen a new caste of revolutionary leaders who were often little better than bandits. The revolutionary army, with its five hundred generals and its hundred thousand soldiers, was the master of the country; and though it had professed to be fighting to abolish praetorianism, its officers had rapidly acquired all the vices which, since the days of Iturbide and Santa Anna, had distinguished Mexican militarists. Most of the country had virtually disintegrated into a series of independent sovereign principalities, governed by chieftains who had once been stirred by a genuine hatred of tyranny and had ended by wanting only power and plunder for themselves and their henchmen.'

In Mexico City the masses were both miserable and angry. The workers were being paid in *Carrancista* money, which was being printed in ever-increasing quantities. Food was very scarce, and prices were marked up not in *Carrancista* currency, but in gold pesos. The workers of Mexico City and a number of other cities, such as the oil port of Tampico, began at last to stir themselves. The organised workers of the capital — and particularly the *Casa del Obrero Mundial* — had been friendly towards, first, Obregon, and then, to some extent, towards Carranza. Now they were disenchanted.

Late in May, 1916, the capital's electrical and tram workers went on strike, and demanded a 'living wage.' They received a slight increase, but as the value of the currency continued to rapidly decline, they were soon worse off than before. At the end of June, the Federation of Labour syndicates of the Federal District and Mexico City called a general strike. The capital and its environs were paralysed. Carranza ordered the strike leaders to be jailed, and declared that they would be tried on the basis of the much-hated law of 1862. Realising that this law — which was intended by Juarez to punish people aiding an enemy during war — was not applicable to a strike, Carranza, on August 1, dictated an even harsher decree, imposing the death penalty for 'inciting' strikes in factories, industrial plants and public services. The decree even included merely discussing strike action. Luis Morones, one-time friend of Obregon who had organised the 'Red Battalions,' together with another trade union leader, Ernesto Velasco, were sentenced to death for their part in the strike, though after remaining in jail without trial for over eighteen months, they were released. Another well-known trade union organiser in Tampico, Jose Barrangan Hernandez, was arrested and executed by *Carrancistas* in that city. Troops occupied the electrical workers' union headquarters. And Don Venustiano, like Don Porfirio before him, also closed down the *Casa del Obrero Mundial* as it had now served its purpose.

But the *Zapatistas* were still resisting Carranza's onslaught only a few kilometres to the south of the capital . . . .

IN September, 1916, Carranza called for an election of deputies to the Constituent Congress, which was to meet on December 1, in Queretaro. He had made up his mind to stand for the presidency, though as an interim president he was inelligible for election anyway. Such trifles did not worry the 'constitutionalist,' Carranza. Only *Carrancista* candidates would be allowed to stand for Congress.

The Constitutionalist Congress was convened on November 25, with all the *Carrancistas* calling themselves liberals, though some were far more 'liberal' than others; indeed, some of the 'left' *Carrancistas* were dubbed Jacobins, which in some ways they resembled. Naturally, the 'Jacobins' did most of the talking, but were generally out-voted by the more conservative 'liberals.'

In his opening speech on December 1, Carranza said that the old constitution of 1857 was abstract and of no use in 1916. He proposed a new constitution – which was equally vague. Some of the delegates insisted on amending it. It was agreed that the propagation of 'religious cults' – which really meant Roman Catholicism – would be forbidden in schools. Other proposals included the nationalisation of subsoil resources, the provision for a minimum wage, social insurance and profit sharing. Also accepted was a clause recognising the private ownership of property.

Much of the Queretaro Constitution was more an expression of 'revolutionary asperations' rather than a practical plan for action. Carranza, therefore, accepted the document, swearing to obey and enforce it. He also began, discreetly at first, his campaign for the presidency.

On February 5, 1917, Carranza ordered the promulgation of the new constitution. He then issued a call for an election to be held on March 11 — an election in which he would be the principle candidate for the presidency. He did not return to Mexico City. It would, he said, seem somewhat incongruous for him to sit in the National Palace, holding the reins of government as 'First Chief,' and at the same time conduct an election legalising his grip on those reins. So, instead, he travelled about the country — politicking.

The election was quite uneventful. About three million Mexicans (out of a total population of around eleven million) were qualified to vote. Carranza claimed that almost half the electorate went to the polls; but official returns suggested that less than 250,000 actually voted. Of those, 197,385 votes went to Carranza. Most of the rest went to Obregon who got 40,000 and Pablo Gonzalez who received just over 11,000, neither of whom stood or campaigned for office. It was another typical Mexican election.

On May 1, 1917, Venustiano Carranza was formerly installed as president. The *Carrancista* 'revolution' was over. Villa was little more than a nuisance; Felix Diaz was hovering in the wings, but was of no account, and Obregon, weary and disillusioned, had retired. That only left Emiliano Zapata.

DURING 1917 and 1918, Gildardo Magana came into his own as Zapata's main adviser and diplomatic 'fixer.'

Magana was not from Morelos. Originally, he came from Zamora in the state of Michoacan on the Pacific Coast, but his family had moved from that very conservative and fanatically Catholic state to Mexico City. The Maganas were of bourgeois origin, and were liberal Catholics. Gildardo first became a *Maderista* and then, some time later, a *Zapatista*. He was, however, a moderate man who yearned for unity among all revolutionary and, in some instances, not-so-revolutionary factions. At twenty-six, Gildardo Magana soon eclipsed both Manuel Palafox and Antonio Diaz Soto y Gama within the *Zapatista* camp. This was largely due to the changed circumstances, and adverse conditions, in Morelos and the south.

Carranza, like those before him, had not been able to defeat the men and women of Morelos, and he had not destroyed *Zapatismo* either; but Morelos and its people were in a very bad way indeed, and the active *Zapatistas* — who now numbered, at the most, around 10,000 — were very hard-pressed. Hence, Zapata's need of a political fixer of ability. So, he encouraged Magana, though he was far from

144

happy about the arrangement or the situation generally.

In July, 1917, the *Zapatista* headquarters authorised the publication of *A Toast to Alvaro Obregon* in honour of his recent stand against Carranza. In mid-August, Magana sent greetings to Pancho Villa. He also began corresponding with the *Carrancista* military commander in Puebla, General Castro. Later in July they met. The meeting resulted in a furious exchange of shots; and Magana retired to Tlaltizapan to report the episode to Emiliano.

Once again, government forces began an offensive against the Liberation Army, and by November most of the Morelense towns were in government hands. But, as in the past, the anti-*Zapatista* campaign soon got bogged down. Magana continued his diplomacy. A number of very minor anti-*Carrancista* revolts broke out in Veracruz, Coahuila, Hidalgo and elsewhere. Magana wrote to various groups, urging them to unite with all the 'healthy elements' of the revolution. The *Zapatista* headquarters issued two more manifestos – *To The Revolutionaries* and *To The People* – both calling for unity in the struggle against Carranza. But the other rebellions all failed or soon fizzled out before the end of January, 1918.

Again, Morelos was on its own.

About the same time, Magana even approached Carranza. He said that the *Zapatistas* wanted a cease-fire, and a promise of civil guarantees to the towns and *pueblos* of the south. Zapata, said Magana, was prepared to negotiate. Carranza, however, ignored Magana's overtures.

On February 27, 1918, the *Zapatista* headquarters put out another statement attacking Carranza and the government for deceiving the people; and the *Zapatista* newspaper, *El Sur*, accused Carranza of deceiving not only the *peones* but also the industrial workers with his labour legislation. On the one hand, said the paper on April 20, Carranza conceded all sorts of rights to the workers, while on the other he declared that only those actions which sought to harmonise labour and capital were legal. By giving the government the option to declare strikes illegal, continued the paper, Carranza had effectively destroyed the right to strike, and thereby had placed the workers at the mercy of the capitalists.

Meanwhile, Magana began to woo the supporters of Don Porfirio's nephew, Felix Diaz. This was a dangerous move, as Don Felix was even more reactionary than Don Venustiano himself. But for some time, Magana had been cooperating with the Puebla *Felicistas*. Indeed it was almost a necessity. He would ally himself with almost any insurgent group. So desperate were the *Zapatistas* that, in their head-

145

quarters' communications and negotiations with other anti-government factions, they no longer mentioned the *Plan de Ayala*, though they still adhered to its basic principles.

Manuel Palafox was also removed. He was considered far too unconciliatory. It was even rumoured that his sex was changing. He was sent to Tochimilco where, it was hoped, he would do no harm. Magana continued his efforts in diplomacy. He wrote to both the *Felicistas* and the *Villistas*. Then in August, he sent two letters to Obregon, in which he condemned Carranza. He asked Obregon for help. But Obregon did not reply. Nor did he openly rebel against Carranza. Magana's diplomacy came to nothing. In Morelos, things went from bad to worse.

The influenza epidemic had been spreading throughout the world. In early October, 1918, it appeared in Mexico City; it soon spread to Morelos and the south. It was inevitable. Many were starving, and continually on the move. And in the mountain hideouts, the biting winter cold did its worst. Even in some of the towns bodies piled up faster than they could be buried. Through sickness, death and emigration, Morelos lost perhaps twenty-five percent of its population in 1918 alone. No prominent *Zapatista* died, but many of Zapata's headquarters' staff were sick for weeks. Zapata was dangerously short of supplies and ammunition.

It was not, therefore, surprising that, as a last resort, Emiliano was forced to put his trust in Magana. In November, 1918, General Gonzalez began yet another campaign against the *Zapatistas*. After the rains stopped in December, he increased the pressure. With more than 12,000 troops, moving from Cuautla and Jonacatepec, he easily occupied Cuernavaca, Jojutla, Yautepec and Tetecala. Tiny *Zapatista guerrillero* groups tried to resist, but were quickly forced into the hills and mountains. Soon after, Tlaltizapan was captured. Almost all the Morelos chiefs, of whom many were still resisting after almost nine years, were on the run. Even the most indefatigable of them all, the 'independent' Genovevo de la O, could only make the occasional raid against Gonzalez. Zapata was hiding in the mountains, and was moving from camp to camp, a few steps ahead of Gonzalez's men.

CHAPTER XVII

CHINAMECA HACIENDA

PALAFOX, following his dismissal from the Tlaltizapan camp, deserted the *Zapatista* movement altogether. He went to Arenista, where he called upon the chiefs to give up the struggle, and to desert Zapata. He urged them to join a new separatist, agrarian movement under the old *Magonista* slogan of *'tierra y libertad!'*. But none of them joined him.

At the beginning of 1919, Gonzalez appointed a new state governor, Colonel Jose G. Aguila; and in February, leaving his generals in charge of government forces in Morelos, he returned to Mexico City, where he boasted that the south had returned to a 'life of order.' He was largely right. Even Genovevo de la O had agreed to an informal truce. And the trains between Cuautla and Mexico City were no longer being blown up. Nevertheless, neither Emiliano Zapata nor any of the other *Zapatista* chiefs had been killed or captured. Zapata continued to move from one base to another. None of the people betrayed him. And Magana remained.

'It was a strange army, these *Zapatistas*,' says Bertram D. Wolfe on the situation in 1918 and the beginning of 1919. 'It increased and diminished with the planting of the harvest. It shrank with defeats and swelled with victories, almost disappeared with each promise-fed illusion, and reformed mightier than ever with each disillusion of fulfillment. When Federal (that is government) troops surrounded one of its peasant-clad detachments, it simply disappeared, buried its rifles and blended into the surrounding peasantry as it tilled the soil. The danger past, the *Zapatistas* dug up their rifles, counted their cartridges and reassembled. There was at all times a heavy price on Emiliano Zapata's head, but not one of his followers could be bought to betray him.'

But, at last, someone could be found who would . . . .

That man was Colonel Jesus Maria Guajardo, commander of the Fiftieth Regiment of the Mexican Army in Morelos, under General Pablo Gonzalez. He was a half-breed Yaqui, and a native of Coahuilan, who had, at one time, been a *Villista*. He has been described as 'a dashing young colonel with upswept mustaches,' with a reputation for ruthlessness, and a hatred of *peones, rancheros* and, particularly, *'Zapatista* trash,' which he had demonstrated against the peasants of the state of Michoacan. Guajardo relished the opportunity of

147

crushing the *'Zapatista* trash.' And he wanted Zapata's head, and
the 100,000 pesos reward.

The scene was set.

ABOUT the middle of March, 1919, Gonzalez ordered Colonel
Guajardo to attack Zapata in the mountains around Huautla. Zapata
escaped. Shortly after, Gonzalez caught Guajardo in bed, in a *cantina*,
with a 'sixteen-year-old *senorita* of pedigree'. Guajardo escaped out
of a back door, but was later arrested. He was held at Gonzalez's
headquarters' prison in Cuautla. He was to be court-martialled 'for
behaving with drunken insolence in the presence of his superior officer.'
He was also to be indicted in the civil courts for abducting the girl.
His position appeared perilous.

At the same time, a *Zapatista* officer, Eusebio Jauregui, had been
recently captured. He was also imprisoned at Gonzalez's headquarters.
He expected to be shot. But instead of being executed, as was usual,
he was allowed enough freedom to overhear Guajardo complaining
of his treatment by Gonzalez. He also heard him criticise Carranza,
and make vague threats about changing sides. A little later, Guajardo
was able to speak to Jauregui. He explained that he was in a bad way;
and that he was going to be court-martialled, and indicted in a civil
court. He said that, although he was an army officer, his sympathies
were secretly with the poor and oppressed.

'In fact, *mi capitan*, to be quite frank, I propose to desert to Zapata
if, or when, I get out of jail .... My men are with me ....have been
with me for years. They are entirely devoted to me .... they always
follow their *jefe* .... If you will help me to arrange matters with
General Zapata, I will see that your sentence is postponed.'

Jauregui believed Guajardo.

And within hours, Jauregui managed – or was allowed! – to
smuggle the information out to be relayed to Zapata. And within
a few days, his letter was delivered to Zapata. Somewhat surprisingly,
Emiliano took the bait as had obviously been planned; though it
was true that he was badly in need of allies – any allies – and
Guajardo's eight hundred men could quite well alter the balance
of forces in his favour. Zapata also trusted Eusebio Jauregui.
Moreover, many former *Maderistas, Villistas* and even *Carrancistas*
had, at various times, deserted their chiefs or had changed sides.

Zapata wrote a letter to Guajardo on March 21, and arranged for
a courier to deliver it to him. He said: 'Although I do not know the
reasons, I understand that you have had some difficulties with Pablo

Gonzalez, and that you have been treated unjustly. This, and the firm and serene conviction that the arms of the revolution will soon triumph, leads me to write this letter, making a formal and frank invitation to you to join our troops. Among us you will be received with the consideration which you merit.'

The letter, when it arrived was immediately placed before General Gonzalez, who told Guajardo that he was to play along with Zapata. And when caught, he added, Zapata would be publicly executed; and if he resisted, he would be shot on the spot. Anyhow, the actual details could be left to Colonel Guajardo. Gonzalez then released Guajardo from military detention, but let it be known that he was to report regularly at the Cuautla army headquarters. Instructions were given to prepare a reply to Zapata. The *Carrancista* governor of Morelos, Jose G. Aguila, composed it for Guajardo. He wrote:

'I inform you that, due to the great difficulties I have had with Pablo Gonzalez I am disposed to collaborate with you if I am given sufficient guarantees for myself and my men, improving my circumstances as a revolutionist. I have sufficient elements of war — munitions, weapons and cavalry under my orders, as well as other elements ready to follow me, awaiting my decision. I await your letter; please keep this delicate matter secret.'

The letter was then sent to Zapata.

By April 1, Emiliano replied, saying that he was agreeably surprised at Guajardo's response, but he must prove his loyalty to the cause. Zapata first asked Guajardo to attack a renegade *Zapatista* group led by Victoriano Barcenas — a man notorious for his cruelty — of whom a delegation of villagers had complained that they had raided the village, raped some of the girls, hanged a number of the old men and looted their entire stores of corn. Zapata suggested that Guajardo attack the Barcenas group on April 3, near Jonacatepec, where they were encamped. He said that they should be disarmed and held at Guajardo's headquarters, by then at Chinameca *hacienda*, while Barcenas should be sent to Zapata, who was at Tepehuaje *rancho*.

Colonel Guajardo — or perhaps, it was again governor Aguilar — replied immediately to Zapata, saying that he could not move for a few days, as a shipment of arms and ammunition, as well as 10,000 pesos, was due for delivery in Cuautla between April 6 and April 10 — and he needed the arms, and money, before rebelling. It would be a shame to let them go, he told Zapata. He did, however, offer to send Zapata some food and other non-military supplies. He also mentioned that he now had daily mule trains operating between Chinameca and Cuautla, bringing supplies. Emiliano replied again to Guajardo, urging him not to delay too long. He also sent an aide, Feliciano Palacios, to Guajardo's base camp at the *hacienda*, with instructions to negotiate for supplies from the mule trains.

Palacios did not detect anything suspicious in the Chinameca camp. Guajardo informed him that there were over five hundred men at his camp ready to attack the government-held town of Jonacatepec, once the ammunition had arrived. Other bogus 'defectors' also promised to attack a number of other government-held towns. Zapata was getting impatient, but accepted Guajardo's word. By April 7, all was ready for an 'attack' on Jonacatepec. The ammunition had arrived, he told Zapata. To divert attention from Morelos, a few *Zapatista* groups, who were beginning to become active again, attacked Cholula in the state of Puebla the same day. And that night in Cuautla, Guajardo made final preparations for his 'attack' on Jonacatepec; and as he left Cuautla, the *Zapatista* prisoner, Eusebio Jauregui, was able to send Zapata a message to the effect that Guajardo was about to leave.

The next day, Colonel Guajardo 'attacked' Jonacatepec. The town was only defended by a small body of *Carrancista* troops, who had already been informed by Pablo Gonzalez what to expect. A sham battle was fought. Both sides either used blank cartridges, or shot high. But despite the precautions, twelve of the 'defenders' and seven of the 'attackers' were accidently killed. Nevertheless, that made it look better for Guajardo. The garrison then withdrew, slowly and in good order, over open plains where any genuine attackers could have annihilated them. Later the same day, Guajardo was able to round up all the renegade *Zapatistas* — except their leader, Barcenas, whom he allowed to escape! — and had all fifty of them lined up against a wall and shot.

Calmly, he said: 'Now tell General Zapata how his loyal and devoted ally, Colonel Guajardo, deals with those who offend the *Zapatista* law.'

When Zapata heard the news he was stunned. It was not so much the men who should have been executed, but, if he was found guilty by a *Zapatista* tribubal, the renegade officer, Victoriano Barcenas. Emiliano was, however, pleased with Guajardo's 'victory' at Jonacatepec.

EMILIANO Zapata went on April 9, with a number of his aides to Pastor Station, a small rail stop on the Interoceanic line about thirty kilometres south of Jonacatepec, to await the arrival of Colonel Guajardo.

A number of *Zapatista* 'spies' had heard rumours of a trick, but Zapata restrained his normal suspicions. About the middle of the afternoon, Guajardo and Zapata met at Pastor Station. The meeting was quite cordial. Zapata only had thirty men, but Guajardo had almost all his troops — probably five hundred, as well as machine-guns. Nevertheless, he was aware that other *Zapatistas* were in the vicinity. Emiliano congratulated Guajardo on his victory at Jonacatepec. And Guajardo then introduced each of his officers to Zapata, and had them mount their horses — and ride slowly past him. He invited Zapata to chose one of his horses — and take it as a gift. A clever move, indeed. Zapata chose a fine sorrel known as Golden Ace; and offered Guajardo his sincere felicitations.

Colonel Guajardo and General Zapata rode about four kilometres alone together to the *pueblo* of Tepalcingo, where Zapata invited Guajardo to join him later for supper with other Morelos chiefs. But Guajardo declined, saying that he had a stomach ache. He gave Zapata an *abrazo*, and then told him that he wanted to return to Chinameca *hacienda* to make sure that Gonzalez did not take his stores. Arrangements were made for Emiliano to visit Guajardo at the *hacienda* the next day, where Guajardo would offer Zapata a *fiesta* in honour of their alliance. They could discuss their future strategy against Carranza, added Guajardo.

Zapata and his escort encamped in the hills just outside Tepalcingo where, shortly after, he was visited by a woman friend* who had just come from Cuautla, where she had heard of a plot to kill Zapata.

Emiliano still had some misgivings, but he was prepared to give Guajardo a chance. He did, however, remark to a comrade: 'I will not regret dying . . . . My mission will soon be over, but those who survive will complete what I cannot do . . . . The seed is planted, and will surely bear fruit.'

About another hundred-and-fifty *Zapatista* reinforcements arrived at the camp during the evening.

Emiliano went to bed 'with the woman he loved.'† He had a rest-

*According to some writers, this was the Romanian journalist, Helene Pontipirani, whom Zapata had previously met.
† This may again have been Helene Pontipirani, but we do not know for certain.

151

less night. Just after 3 a.m. he suddenly arose, dressed and, before dawn, saddled and mounted his new horse, Golden Ace, and with an escort of thirty men, rode out towards the *hacienda* of Chinameca. The *hacienda* lay along the Cuautla river about sixty kilometres away, just below Villa de Ayala. The *hacienda* of Chinameca had been the first *hacienda* that Zapata had attacked in 1911.

It was raining steadily. Then the rain suddenly stopped. The night air was cool and fresh.

Shortly after sunrise, Zapata and his escort arrived near Villa de Ayala. They rested awhile. A little after 8.30, Zapata and his men came down from the hills to Chinameca. Surrounded by his staff officers, Guajardo met Zapata at the wide gates of the *hacienda*. He was extremely cordial. Outside the *hacienda* buildings, and against the front walls, stood a number of company stores. In one of them, Guajardo and Zapata began to confer. They discussed the subject of ammunition and other supplies. Then, suddenly, they were interrupted by a number of Guajardo's scouts, who announced that government troops were approaching from the north. Guajardo said that he would place himself under General Zapata's command.

Emiliano quickly directed Guajardo to guard the *hacienda* with his forces, while he and his men would go and reconnoitre. He knew the area well. But after looking for some time, he could see no troops approaching. Nevertheless, he posted lookouts in the surrounding hills. It was almost 1.30 p.m. Only Guajardo's men and Zapata's aide, Palacios, were inside the *hacienda*. Emiliano waited outside for awhile. Then, Guajardo sent a message to Zapata, inviting him to join him, first, for a *copita*, and later, a *fiesta*. Finally convinced that there were no government troops in the area, Zapata accepted. It was 2.30 p.m. Selecting only ten men, and mounting his horse, Emiliano Zapata set out on the one-kilometre ride through the *hacienda* grounds towards the fortress-like *casco*.

With his escort just behind him, riding three abreast, Zapata entered the open courtyard gates. Guajardo's men had formed ranks on three sides of the *patio*. They stood to attention. Guajardo and his officers stood on the steps of the *portal*. As Zapata passed through the shadow of the gates, Colonel Guajardo raised his sword. A bugler put his bugle to his lips, and sounded the 'Honour Call.' As the last note died away, Guajardo lowered his sword. As Guajardo's men presented arms, every third rifle butt went to a shoulder. They fired point blank at Emiliano and his escort, without giving them a chance to draw their pistols. Zapata stood up in his stirrups, and instinctively turned his horse. His hand went down, but his pearl handled Colt remained in its holster. There was a second volley. Zapata pitched from his saddle, and crashed to the ground.

Riddled with bullets, his bloody body lay dead in the courtyard. . . .

Most of Zapata's comrades fell with him, but three managed to escape and ride out of the gates. Inside the *hacienda* building, Palacio heard the shooting; he asked Guajardo, who had just entered, what it was. 'This' replied Guajardo, and, pulling out his pistol, he shot him through the head. Palacio fell dead at his feet.

WITHIN seconds of Zapata's murder, Guajardo ordered his men to drag the corpse into the *hacienda* building. And less than two hours later, Guajardo, fearful of revenge, tied Zapata's body, with its white shirt and dark grey *charro* trousers soaked in blood, on to a mule and, leading his column of men, left the *hacienda* for the safety of Cuautla.

At 7.30 that evening, the column passed through Villa de Ayala. Guajardo telephoned General Pablo Gonzalez the news. 'I'm bringing in Zapata,' he said. Two hours later, he arrived in Cuautla. Gonzalez and all his officers were there to meet him. Zapata's corpse was cut from the mule and dumped on to the ground. Gonzalez shone a torch into Zapata's face for all to see. The body was then taken to the local Municipal Palace; and the wretched *Zapatista* prisoner, Eusebio Jauregui, who had unwittingly assisted in the murder of his comrade and chief, was asked to formally identify the body. This he did. His statement was taken down for the official report. Then, having served his purpose, Jauregui was taken outside and immediately shot. Later, photographs of the dead Emiliano were taken.

General Gonzalez telegraphed Carranza to inform him that Guajardo had carried out *el movimiento preparado*; he also recommended that Colonel Guajardo be promoted to the rank of general. Gonzalez's official message read:

With the greatest satisfaction, I have the honour of informing you that Colonel Jesus Guajardo and his forces have just arrived bringing the cadaver of Emiliano Zapata who, for so many years, was chief of the revolution in the south and the irreducible rebellion in this region.'

Carranza replied:

'I have received with satisfaction your report telling of the death of Emiliano Zapata as a result of the plan executed so well by Colonel Jesus Guajardo. Because of Colonel Guajardo's conduct, I have dictated a promotion in grade for Colonel Guajardo and his officers.'

Colonel Guajardo duly became a general, much to the consterna-

Colonel Jesus Guajardo of Carranza's army, who betrayed and murdered Emiliano Zapata. (From a drawing by a native artist.)

tion of his fellow officers. He also received 50,000 gold pesos – half the original sum offered for the capture or death of Zapata – for his treachery. He, like Gonzalez and Carranza, was, however, well-satisfied. But he was not to enjoy the success for very long.

For two days, following the return to Cuautla, Gonzalez arranged a public exhibition, according to custom, of Zapata's cadaver, by then dressed in a clean grey *charro* suit and a new white shirt, and placed upon a rough *catafalque*, in Cuautla's *plaza*. Tens of thousands of ordinary *peones, rancheros, and campesinos*, including Zapata's two sisters, Jesucita and Luz, came to pay their respects to the dead 'Miliano, the *ranchero* from San Miguel Anencuilco, who had become Supreme Chief of the Liberation Army of the South and Centre. One by one they filed past the open coffin. Some just stared; many wept; others trembled from head to foot, and a few crossed themselves. The news of Zapata's death soon spread throughout Morelos, and then to the rest of the south and, finally, throughout Mexico and even abroad.

Someone painted on a wall in large black letters Zapata's well-known saying: 'It is better to die on your feet than live on your knees.' And Marcianito Silva, the folk-singer and guitarist who had been with Zapata, composed a *corrido*:

> '*Adios,* forest of Ajusco,
> *Adios*, hills of Jilguero,
> *Adios*, you caves and mountains,
> That knew our *guerrero.*'

Gonzalez had a movie camera record the funeral at the Cuautla public cemetery on the Saturday, just three days after Zapata had been shot. Mexico City's newspapers screamed that the notorious '*Atila del Sur*' was no more. *Zapatismo*, they claimed, was also dead. And General Gonzalez boasted that *Zapatismo* was finished.

But they were wrong. *Zapatismo* was not finished.
And, indeed, many asserted that Emiliano was not dead either. Many would not believe that 'their 'Miliano' had been killed. For decades, they declared that, on dark nights, Emiliano Zapata could be seen in the hills and mountains of Morelos, clad in white and riding a fine white horse. For them, he still lived!

And within a year, the Liberation Army of the south was on the move again, stronger than it had been for years.

155

CHAPTER XVIII

AFTERMATH

THROUGHOUT 1918 and 1919, Venustiano Carranza managed to stay in the presidential saddle without actually doing anything much. The enormous floods of paper money finally became completely worthless; and gold and silver re-emerged as the only legal tender. But very little of it reached the workers, and even less the *peones*.

In May, 1918, the *Carrancista* governor of Coahuila organised a convention of labour leaders. And the government paid the delegates' travelling expenses to Saltillo, where the convention was held. Carranza hoped that they would support him. But things did not go the way the government or the good governor had planned. Luis Morones, Alvaro Obregon's old friend, soon dominated the proceedings. Previously, he had formed a *Grupo Accion*, which later emerged as the nucleus of a Labour Party. The convention itself formed the *Confederacion Regional Obrera Mexicana*, which abandoned the old, and rather ineffective, syndicalism. CROM soon became a federation of largely craft unions on the American Federation of Labour model; and its policies were tightly controlled by the *Grupo Accion*. Within a year, CROM and the new Labour Party nominated Obregon as their presidential candidate.

Don Venustiano's term of office was to officially end in 1920. He knew that he could not be re-elected. But he did not want to see Obregon become president. So, he decided to back a certain 'Meester' Ignacio Bonillas, the Mexican Ambassador to the United States, of whom no one in Mexico had ever heard. Carranza spent two million gold pesos of government money in promoting the Bonillas candidacy.

Obregon accepted the CROM's nomination, and criticised Carranza for not pacifying the country. He began an energetic campaign. But he was increasingly harassed by Carranza's officials. His supporters were also victimised. As this did not discourage the *Obregonistas*, Carranza staged a plot against Obregon. He accused him of supporting an anti-government conspiracy. Obregon was called upon to testify in a Mexico City court. His friends advised him not to go, but he decided to obey the court. On the first day of the trial of a *Felicista* 'conspirator', Obregon denied any knowledge of the matter; but he was ordered to remain in the capital for a further appearance. He was kept under constant police surveillance. And as the number of police trailing him increased, he decided that he must get away before he was arrested or murdered.

Disguised as a railroad worker and accompanied by an old friend, General Benjamin Hill, Obregon managed to escape to the state of Guerrero.

By February, 1920, anti-Carranza feeling was building up in many parts of the country. Plutarco Elias Calles, the Minister of Industry, Commerce and Labour, resigned from the government, and went to Sonora where he 'declared war' upon Carranza. Benjamin Hill made his way to Morelos, where he joined the *Zapatistas*. By the end of April, rebellions against Carranza had broken out in Chiapas, Chihuahua, Hidalgo, the Federal District, Michoacan, Nuevo Leon, Oaxaca, San Luis Potosi, Tabasco, Veracruz, Zacatecas — and, of course, Morelos. By the end of May, even the notorious *Carrancista* general, Pablo Gonzalez, declared himself to be in revolt.

Carranza's days were numbered.

He decided, as he had done previously, to go to Veracruz. But he did not go alone. Altogether, about 10,000 people started out — in eighteen trains. They included the wives, mistresses and children of Carranza's remaining supporters. And they took with them all the gold and silver in the Treasury, furniture from the National Palace, government printing presses, a number of aircraft which they had disassembled and even horses from the Palace stables. But they were doomed to failure. Most of the carriages lacked airbrakes, and some of the engines were short of coal or water, or both. There were insufficient railwaymen to run the trains, as most train crews were *Obregonistas* or *Magonistas*.

Trouble began almost immediately, when at Villa de Guadalupe a group of *Zapatistas* sent a locomotive from the opposite direction on the same line, charged with dynamite, head-on into the first train carrying *Carrancista* troops. Over two hundred were killed. The track was cleared and repaired. They then proceeded. The somewhat depleted convoy of trains continued on its way to Veracruz, only to be attacked at various places along the line. But when the *Carrancistas* arrived at Aljibes, they found that the track ahead was completely destroyed. For them, it was the end of the line. Carranza decided to lead the remnants of his party on foot through northern Puebla, and on to San Luis Potosi, where, he hoped, he could reorganise. Carranza and his party — still carrying millions of gold and silver pesos — plodded on for five days over some of the roughest terrain in all

Mexico, often in torrential rain. At last they encamped in the tiny Indian village of Tlaxacalantongo. There was no food in the village.

During the night of May 19, Carranza and his party were suddenly attacked by a group of 'bandits' shouting '*Viva* Obregon!'. Carranza was shot in the hip, and died shortly afterwards. Those *Carrancistas* who had not been killed or captured, fled. Most of the loot was never recovered. The leader of the 'bandits', Rodolfo Herrero, is reported to have died a very rich man!

ZAPATISMO did not die with the death of Emiliano Zapata. Within five days of his assassination about thirty *Zapatista* chiefs and head-quarters' secretaries, including Jesus Capistran, Gildardo Magana, Francisco Mendoza and Genovevo de la O, signed and issued a new *Manifesto to the People of Mexico*, in which they recalled that, after the deaths of Hidalgo and Morelos, the struggle for independence and against oppression had still continued; and that they, and the people, must continue their struggle until they too triumphed.

Within a few weeks, many of the chiefs, and the *peones*, began a new campaign against local *Carrancista* officials, and the occupying forces. Army officers particularly were hunted down and shot.

Nevertheless, the *Zapatistas* were far from being united. They had yet to decide who would take Zapata's place as Supreme Chief of the Liberation Army of the South and Centre. The two main contenders were Magana and Mendoza. Magana was the fixer, but Mendoza had been active since the end of 1910. Magana acted quickly by sending out invitations to all the chiefs to assemble in a junta, and elect a new supreme chief as soon as possible. But Mendoza refused to co-operate. He said that he was prepared to attend, but he kept putting off the journey.

By the end of May, many of the chiefs had proposed Gildardo Magana; and he even proposed himself, saying Emiliano had always considered disputes within the movement to be treason. But Magana did not press the issue. He decided to wait. Mendoza, therefore, assumed the position of Supreme Chief of the Liberation Army. But he received little support from outside his own area. Meanwhile, Genovevo de la O began to correspond with a number of *Obregonistas*; and the former *Zapatista* Manuel Palafox exchanged notes with leading *Felicistas*. Everyone who was opposed to Don Venustiano seemed to be looking for allies.

Eventually, on September 4, 1919, at Capistran's camp in the hills near Huautla, the *Zapatista* junta assembled. It was well-attended, with over thirty chiefs present. Its sole object was to elect a new supreme chief. Various names were proposed and seconded. They included Magana, Mendoza, Capistran, Soto y Gama and de la O. Each was voted upon. After a number of ballots, Magana received a clear majority of eighteen over Capistran. All chiefs then swore to respect the majority decision. And so Gildardo Magana became Supreme Chief of the Liberation Army of the South and Centre – but in name only.

He immediately went to Mexico City where he had secret talks with Carranza. Don Venustiano asked him what he wanted, and he replied: 'Only guarantees.' For the first time for years, many of the Morelos chiefs were safe in their own areas – they had just received amnesties – yet Magana, who had 'fixed' everything, was virtually under house arrest in Mexico City. He was the guarantor. Genovevo de la O and Francisco Mendoza remained with their men in the hills, and refused to accept Carranza's amnesty. A few *hacendados* returned to Morelos.

In January, 1920, Magana managed to escape from Mexico City, and became an outlaw in the Puebla mountains. But, once again, less than twelve months after Zapata's death, the Liberation Army began to reform. The headquarters at Tlaltizapan was reorganised. De la O arranged for supplies, and by mid-March there were over 10,000 *Zapatistas* under arms again. They decided for tactical reasons to throw in their lot with Alvaro Obregon. The *Obregonista* general, Benjamin Hill, was welcomed by Genovevo de la O to his camp at La Cima. Most of the amnestied chiefs returned to the fold.

The *Obregonista* revolt was now sweeping the country like a prairie fire. Of course, many veteran *Zapatistas* were quite naturally suspicious of Obregon's intentions, but, with Magana, they decided to give him conditional support. Obregon made a brief visit to Morelos where, together with a rather taciturn de la O, he addressed a large meeting from the balcony of Mrs. King's Bella Vista hotel in Cuernavaca.

The *Carrancistas* fought a few rear-guard actions, but at the beginning of May, 1920, the Liberation Army of the South, led jointly by Genovevo de la O and Benjamin Hill moved in an enormous column towards Mexico City. And on May 9, Alvaro Obregon, riding next to Genovevo de la O, entered the capital in triumph. Four days later, Magana and Soto y Gama arrived in the city, in the words of John Womack Jr., 'in dark suits and hats now like proper dignitaries, to be photographed showered in their friends' confetti, dumbly gripping ceremonial boquets.'

On June 2, over 30,000 people, made up largely of *Zapatistas*, paraded through Zocalo and past the National Palace. Watching from the balcony, were, among others, Magana, Soto y Gama and Genovevo de la O. But like Zapata before him, de la O looked glum and suspicious. He alone was not happy. He had seen it all before. He allowed his photograph to be taken; but, again like Zapata, he frowned at the camera. He refused to attend any functions or banquets. But he did agree to accept the title of Divisional General of the Army of the South, which was to be officially incorporated into the newly-constituted National Army of the Republic of Mexico. He probably realised that, on that day, the Liberation Army of the South and Centre ceased to be.

On the afternoon of June 1, De la Huerta went to the Chamber of Deputies, where he was sworn in as interim president. In July, he announced the official retirement of Pancho Villa, who was given a large *hacienda* for his 'services to the revolution.' Don Porfirio's nephew, Felix Diaz, was allowed to go to America. General Guajardo, who had so treacherously murdered Zapata, started to criticise and attack the new government. He was arrested and, to the satisfaction of many *Zapatistas*, was executed on the orders of the governor of the state of Nuevo Leon. General Pablo Gonzalez was also found guilty of treason, and he too was sentenced to death. He, however, was reprieved and allowed to go to the Untied States.

The presidential election was held on September 5, 1920. There were a number of candidates from various groups, including a Catholic party and a small Republican party; but Obregon, with CROM and Labour support, was the main contender. On October 26, he was announced the winner with 1,132,751 votes against 47,422 for the Catholic and Republican candidates. No one appears to have accused Obregon of fraud or intimidation. 'Precisely at midnight between November 30 and December 1, in the Chamber of Deputies, Alvaro Obregon raised his one arm and was sworn into office,' writes an observer. He was the twelfth president in less than a decade.

After ten years of revolution and civil war, Mexico was in a very poor way indeed. The power of the *hacendados* and *cientificos* had been largely broken; but the people were both physically and mentally exhausted. Even the men and women of Morelos had had more than enough.

* *

APPENDIX

THE EJIDOS AND THE LAND QUESTION

PEOPLE have lived in Mexico a long time. Their roots are planted deep in the soil. They are part of the great migration that crossed the Bering Straight from Siberia, fought the bitter cold of the Fourth Glaciation which covered much of Asia and North America, and then moved south.

No one knows exactly when what is now called Mexico began to be populated, but the anthropologist, William Howells, reports the finding of a human skeleton, together with the skeletons of two mammoths at Tepexpan, northeast of Mexico City, in a glacial layer at least 12,000 years old.[1] Hand-made artifacts have been found at Valsequillo in central Mexico dated from 20,000 years ago.[2] Settled farming communities existed in Mexico from about 7,000 BC. By 6,000 BC beans were being raised, and 1,000 years later, squash. Corn, cultivated since at least 5,500 BC, became Mexico's major crop around 1,500 BC.[3]

The first Mexicans of whom there are records, lived in the Valley of Mexico and surrounding areas, including what is now called Morelos. They settled there about one century BC. They occupied permanent villages, and subsisted chiefly on the products of their common fields. They produced sufficient for their needs. They appear to have been peaceful. Their irrigated lands and artificial island gardens were enormously productive, and crops were planted several times a year.[4]

About AD 400, a new people spread into the Valley of Mexico from Puebla and beyond Morelos. These have been called Toltecs or Master Builders. Tenochtitlan was their capital. The Toltecs have been described as great architects. 'They were skilled likewise in agriculture, cultivating corn, cotton, beans, chili peppers and all other domesticated plants known to Mexico,' comments George C. Vailant.[5] They held a market every twenty days in Cuernavaca and many other towns. They prospered and multiplied. But by AD 1,000, Toltec culture began to decline, and shortly after came to an end.

From then until about 1,300, Mexican society was chaotic, resulting in a mixture of cultures, and eventually giving rise to what has generally been called Aztec civilisation. This is not the place for a detailed account of the development of Mexican society and the ultimate dominance of the Aztec Confederacy in the Valley of Mexico and southwards to Puebla and the Valley of Morelos. Briefly, Henry

Bamford Parkes observes that the Aztecs' 'cultural level was roughly equivalent to that of the Egyptian Pharaohs and the priest-kings of Chaldaea, or the Jewish people under Joshua and the Judges. Society was still theocratic; the gods were, for the most part, still tribal deities and had not yet been universalised, nor had the individual been freed from priestly control.'[6]

What we are interested in, however, is the Mexican Indians' attitude towards the land and land-ownership, from early times, through the Aztec period, the Spanish Conquest, and right up into the present century – particularly in central Mexico, including Morelos, where the mass of the population of Mexico lived.

THE original hunting tribes of Mexico, as elsewhere, had no conception of landed property. Hunting and fishing was practised jointly, and the produce shared in common. The idea of private, or even family, ownership of land developed very slowly indeed, even when the Indians ceased to lead a nomadic existence and lived in villages or *pueblos*. Indeed, the Mexican Indians' attitude towards the land and land-ownership changed very little over the centuries.

Of the situation in the fifteenth century, Parkes remarks :

'The mass of the people cultivated the land. Land was not held as private property. Ownership belonged to the tribe or to some smaller unit within it. Each family, however, was alloted a piece of land which it cultivated independently. Certain lands were reserved for the expenses of the government and the support of the priests, these lands being cultivated by the common people.'[7]

But in the areas dominated by the Aztec Confederation, there began to emerge to a small extent a form of peasant slavery or *peonage* over members of some of the subject tribes. Nevertheless, of the Aztecs, Lewis Henry Morgan writes: 'The Aztec and their Confederate tribes still held their lands in common (and) lived in large households composed of a number of related families.'[8] The majority of the people possessed some personal property, 'but land belonged to the tribe, and only its produce to the individual.'[9] Indeed, 'agriculture was the basis of Aztec life, and corn , *zea mays*, was the chief food plant. The cultivation of plants ensured a food supply near at hand, which was not subject to the fluctuations of game, and thereby enabled man to take thought for the morrow. The clan system recognised that the fruits of the land supported the tribe. Therefore, it was only natural that the tribe should own and control the land which supported its members.'[10]

Beyond the Valley of Mexico the situation was very similar.

'The people of the provinces,' notes William H. Prescott, 'were distributed into *calpulli*, or tribes, who held their lands of the neighbourhood in common. Officers of their own appointment parcelled out these lands among several families of the *capulli*; and on the extinction or removal of a family its lands reverted to common stock, to be again distributed. The individual proprietor held no power to alienate them. The laws regulating these matters were very precise, and had existed ever since the occupation of the country by the Aztecs.'[11]

Land, therefore, was all-important to the Mexican Indian, but it was not the private possession of any one person. In a sense, it belonged to all and, at the same time, it belonged to no one. Of course, the colonisation of Mexico by the Spaniards often changed such relationships and behaviour-patterns — but not all at once or without resistance and conflict, however. Indeed, at the end of the last century, Peter Kropotkin says that 'it is well known that many tribes of Brazil, Central America and Mexico used to cultivate their fields in common.'[12]

And Ricardo Flores Magon wrote in 1906 that 'in Mexico there are some four million Indians who lived, until twenty or twenty-five years ago, in communities that held land, water and woods in common. Mutual aid was the rule in these communities and authority made itself felt only when the rent collector made his periodic appearance, or when the *rurales* came in search of recruits for the army . . . . All had a right to the land, the water for irrigation, the forest was for cutting timber, and the timber was used in the construction of cabins. Ploughs passed from hand to hand, as did the yoke of oxen. Each family cultivated its special strip of land, which was calculated as being sufficient to produce what the family required; and the work of weeding and harvesting the crop was done in common, the entire community uniting to get in Pedro's crop today, Juan's tomorrow, and so on.'[13]

The common lands usually lay on the outer edges of the *pueblo* — hence the term *ejido* (pronounced e-hee-do), which means 'exit' or 'way out.'[14]

THE Spaniards first arrived in Mexican waters in 1517. In 1519, an adventurer by the name of Hernan Cortes sailed to Mexico with five hundred men. First, he established a town, which he called Veracruz. His small force moved inland, and three months later they arrived outside the great Aztec city of Tenochtitlan. Neither he nor any of his men had ever seen such a place before. Babylon in all its glory had never been so splendid!

But Cortes was not able to capture the city, or destroy the Aztec Empire until the end of September, 1521. The Mexicans were not defeated by military conquest but by disease – an epidemic of smallpox, unknown to the Mexicans, brought from Europe by the Spaniards.

Tenochtitlan was systematically destroyed by the Spaniards, and then rebuilt on the model of a Spanish town. It was to become Mexico City. It also became the centre for a series of expeditions, in which the Spaniards founded more towns and cities and, over the next two decades, conquered what was to become New Spain. The Aztecs, as well as all the other peoples of central Mexico, were subjugated; and the Spaniards gained control over enormous tracts of land.

New Spain was largely conquered by private adventurers known as *conquistadors*, whose ambitions were to become rich. The *conquistadors*, however, were firmly controlled by a small group of agents of the Spanish Crown, called *gachupines* – Wearers of Spurs. New Spain was despotically ruled by a Viceroy. The leaders of the Catholic Church, who were all *gachupines*, worked closely with the Viceroy, and were part of the colonial bureaucracy. Their aim was to make Christians of the Mexicans and, thereby, increase the power and wealth of the Church and themselves. Victor Alba describes the system which Spain imposed upon the people of Mexico.

'First, there was the *encomienda*, by which a *conquistador* received a certain amount of land and the Indians who lived on it, in exchange for protecting and Christianising them. The arrangement was in essence a transplant of the feudal system which had long since become moribund in Europe. To save the Indians from being entirely at the mercy of the new lords, and to preserve the ancient system of communal ownership, each Indian village was guaranteed a tract of common farm land – eventually standardised at one square league in size. These *ejidos* .... could not be sold; with these lands, waters, pastures, and woodlands, the Indians were able to subsist. The new lords, however, found ways to make the *encomienda* and the *ejido* profitable for themselves. The former gave them *de facto* domination over the Indians; the latter enabled them to put the Indians to work on the *conquistadors'* lands without pay; since the natives could presumably live on the produce of their *ejidos*.'[15]

The *conquistadors* numbered only a few hundred, and the first generation of colonists a few thousands; yet more than five hundred Spaniards acquired *encomiendas*. At first, the Emperor tried to limit the exploitation of the Indians. He ordered payment for all labour exacted from free and *encomienda* Indians. Indeed, under the rule of the early Viceroys, the conditions of the tribes of central Mexico was not all that worse than it had been under the Aztecs. But in the seventeenth and eighteenth centuries the Indian villages began to suffer from illegal exactions of the *corridors* and from the encroachments of the emerging *creole* landowners. All attempts to protect the *ejidos* were frustrated by corrupt officials. Parkes comments:

'According to Spanish law, all the land of Mexico was ultimately the property of the Crown, and only a royal grant gave legal title to ownership. Since most of the Indian villages had never obtained grants, it was easy for the *creoles* gradually to enlarge the boundaries of their estates, claiming that they were occupying land which belonged to the Crown. After such a usurpation had been tolerated for a considerable period, it was regularised by the government through a *composicion*. .... By a slow process of attrition extending through generations, the relatively small holdings of the original *conquistadors* were gradually enlarged into enormous *haciendas* which covered most of the fertile lands of central Mexico.'[16]

Nevertheless, while Mexico remained part of the Spanish Empire, many *pueblos* preserved a precarious independence. But a considerable proportion of the population – probably almost forty per cent – were compelled to become labourers on the *haciendas*. They were transformed into *peones* – debt-slaves, and their debts were inherited from generation to generation.

The *hacendados* were not interested in improving their methods of production. The Indians were deprived of farm implements and domesticated animals like oxen. Agriculture, therefore, stagnated. Only the comparatively small number of independent small-scale farmers – *rancheros* like the Zapata family for example – could be relied upon to use the land reasonably efficiently. But early in the nineteenth century, a form of 'plantation capitalism' slowly began to emerge. *Haciendas* developed whose aims were purely commercial. By 1810, shortly before Mexico gained her independence, there were 5,000 such estates, of which about one quarter raised livestock. Many of these were, however, in the arid north of the country, and employed very few *peones* or wage-workers. The sugar-producing *haciendas* were generally located in Morelos and the central heartland where the

165

Indian population was most numerous. Yet, in 1810, there were still 4,500 autonomous Indian communities with their *ejidos*.

'Thus,' says Eric R. Wolf, 'Mexico emerged into its period of independence with its rural landscape polarised between large estates on the one hand and Indian communities on the other – units, moreover, which might be linked economically, but which remained set off against each other socially and politically.'[17]

AFTER a long and bittler struggle, Mexico achieved her independence in 1821. 'Independent' Mexico stripped the Church of much of its power, and forced it to sell off considerable amounts of land as well.

But the *hacendados* improved their position. A law passed in 1856, the *Ley Lerdo*, despite the intentions of some of its supporters, made the situation worse for the *peones*. The purposes of the law were to increase government revenues, and to stimulate economic progress. The Church was forbidden to own land, but was to receive payment for its estates. No provision, however, was made for the division of large clerical *haciendas*. Only the already wealthy landowners, therefore, were able to pay the purchase price of the Church lands and the heavy government sales tax. Furthermore, the *Ley Lerdo* ordered the sale of Indian *ejidos* attached to the new Spanish towns, as well as the traditional *peublos*. When many of the land-hungry *mestizos* (people who were part-Indian and part-Spanish) realised that they would not be able to buy the Church lands, they rebelled. The immediate result was a series of minor *mestizo* and Indian revolts throughout central Mexico.

Nevertheless, the number of small *rancheros* did increase, but the most conspicuous result of the *Ley Lerdo* was to increase the concentration of land ownership on a scale hitherto unknown.

By 1889, twenty-nine 'companies' obtained 27.5 million hectares, or fourteen per cent of the total land area of Mexico. And between 1889 and 1894, another six per cent was alienated. 'At the same time,' comments Wolf, 'cultivators who could not show a clear title to their lands were treated as illegal squatters and dispossessed.'[18] By 1900, there were about fifty *haciendas* of over 100,000 hectares. One *hacendado*, Luis Terrazas, owned fifteen *haciendas*, comprising two million hectares, 500,000 head of cattle and 250,000 sheep! Of the situation under Diaz's dictatorship, Gerrit Huizer observes:

'The Mexican Revolution, which began in 1910 and in which the armed peasantry played a crucial role, should be seen against the background of the usurpation of communal lands by large *haciendas*, which took place in the second half of the nineteenth century. Many indigenous communities tried in vain to retain or recover the communal lands of which they had been deprived under legislation which favoured private property. Particularly in the densely populated state of Morelos, the sugar estates expanded at the cost of the communities. The peasants' homes and crops were destroyed to obtain land for sugar cultivation. The peasants affected were forced to work on the estates.'[19]

BETWEEN 1910 and 1920, Mexican society was turned upside down. In a number of states like Morelos and Puebla, the *peones* were able to take much of the land back from the *hacendados*. Nevertheless, in many instances, by 1920, some of the *hacendados* had been able to repossess it again.

During his term as president, Carranza did little more than make promises to the *peones*. Between 1917 and 1920, only 48,000 *peones* received any land. And even these usually possessed neither water, seeds, nor tools, and were forced to work for the local *hacienda*. But Obregon, once elected, made plans for the rural areas. Naturally, they were of a paternalistic nature. In 1923, he had a law passed which gave a parcel of land to each member of an *ejido* as his persona¹ private, property, though the recipient could not sell it.[20] Agrarians like Soto y Gama supported the law enthusiastically. And the landowners received compensation in the form of government bonds. During Obregon's presidency, about 1.2 million hectares were distributed.[21]

In 1924, General Calles was elected president. His regime was more authoritarian than that of Obregon, but he continued to distribute land to the *peones*. He even proclaimed himself the heir of Zapata! What Calles actually did, in an attempt to destroy the power of the local *jefes politicos* and the village *caciques*, was to divide the *ejidos* into individual plots. He also established agricultural banks, but four-fifths of their loans went to the *hacendados*, and not to the ordinary *peones*. Altogether, Calles distributed just under 3.3 million hectares to 1,500 villages.[22]

Calles left office in November, 1928. And he was followed by Portes Gil, whose policies were largely dictated by the ex-president. He lasted less than a year. Nevertheless, during that period, Gil distributed more than one million hectares. In 1930, Ortiz Rubio became president. He lasted two years, during which time he distributed less than 200,000 hectares. He was followed by Alberland Rodriguez, who showed little interest in the land question — or anything else for that matter. Up to the end of 1933, perhaps less than eight million hectares of arable land had been given back to the *peones*. Parkes observes that 'there were still nearly two-and-a-half million families with no land at all. In other words, at the end of twenty years of allegedly revolutionary administration, Mexican rural society was still basically feudal.'[23]

But between 1934 and 1940, during the presidency of Lazaro Cardenas, the rural feudalism, to which Parkes refers, was largely broken. Cardenas was an idealist, but he was also a very practical man and a modernising reformer. In six years, he parcelled out and distributed over twelve million hectares.[24] And he organised an *ejidal* bank, to give credit to the new *rancheros* and farmers. Nevertheless, even by 1940, there were still many large *haciendas* in Mexico. '... the big owners still held more than three times as much land as the *ejidatarios*; sixty per cent of the land was held by less than ten thousand *hacendados*, and there were still three hundred *haciendas* of more than 40,000 hectares apiece'.[25] Fifty per cent of the population engaged in agriculture were still *peones* or wage workers.

WITH the slow, but inevitable, development of industrial capitalism in Mexico, the old as well as the newly-created *ejidos* naturally took on a different form. They tended to become merely co-operative farms, financed largely by the government.

The agricultural bank, which was founded in 1926, soon found itself in a difficult situation due to the duality of its functions. On the one hand, it was supposed to help organise the *ejidatarios* into co-operatives and, at the same time, operate the co-operative farms as non-profit-making concerns; and, on the other hand, it was to make loans to *rancheros* and even some large landowners and *hacendados* producing crops for commercial profit. In 1931, however, the National Agricultural Bank was reorganised. It ceased to lend to the *hacendados*, and only lent money to the *ejidatarios* organised into co-operatives. But in 1934, it was fused with the rural banks; and, once again, these banks were allowed to extend credit to non-*ejidatarios* — but only to small and middle-sized *rancheros*.

Another problem was the legal status of the *ejido*. Originally, the land was, and was to be, held and worked in common. The *ejidatarios* could neither alienate nor mortgage their land. They were to enjoy it 'in usufruct' rather than 'fee simple.' The subject of the right was the community; not the individual. In theory at least, the land belonged to the *pueblos*. Even the tractors — where they existed —

were used in common, and the marketing of the produce was also done collectively. A law of *'Ejido Patrimony'* was promulgated. But by 1935, only about twenty per cent of all *ejidos* had been 'legalised.'

Other methods of 'solving' the agrarian question were, therefore, tried. One of them was the 'colonising projects,' in which, where there was said to be no more land available for distribution in a given area, the *peones* were to be persuaded to move to other regions with more land. It was not a success. [26]

Since 1940, more land has been distributed. But, in the main, government-organised *ejidos* and co-operative farms have not been all that successful or productive, though their establishment — together with an increasing number of *rancheros* — has undoubtedly assisted in breaking the power of the old feudal *hacendados* and many of the planters. Furthermore, the general standard of living (or, perhaps, we should say existence) for the majority of *peones* has not improved all that much. This is borne out by Dr. Josue de Castro, the former Director General of the Food and Agricultural Organisation of the United Nations, who observed in 1952:

'The *ejido* was undoubtedly a step forward for Mexico in the struggle against hunger, but unfortunately, the results fell short of expectation. The Mexican revolutionaries were idealists rather than technicians, and they forgot that mere redistribution of land is not enough. In order to cultivate it adequately, technical and financial resources are also necessary. The result was that the Indians, who were generally unprepared, disorientated, and without adequate technical knowledge, were unable to make proper use of the plots they received. The agrarian reform did not lead to the increase of production or to the indispensable diversification of crops which were needed to raise the national living standards. As proof of this, one may cite the fact that even today Mexico imports appreciable quantities of her basic food element — corn — and still does not have adequate supplies of many protective foods.'[27]

And of the situation, Segovia writes:

'From 1936 onwards there have been attempts, through agrarian reform, to solve the human problems of the rural sector, especially by distributing land to the peasants in the form of *ejidos*. These lands represent thirty-seven per cent of the registered land of the country. Both *ejidos* and smallholdings, owing to population growth, have shown a pronounced tendency to split into uneconomically small sub-holdings; the absolute growth of the rural population has today

(1968) created a situation in which over two million peasants have a statutory right to share in an *ejido*'.[28]

Yet despite all the so-called idealism of the official 'revolutionaries' and politicians, the land, that has been distributed, has been distributed in an authoritarian and paternalistic manner, often as a means of heading off further *Zapatista*-like insurrections and struggles, as well as a method of destroying feudal land ownership in the countryside. Such schemes – at least for the *peones* – were bound to fail. In fact, in the main, even during Cardenas' presidency, government policy has consistently been to encourage *rancheros* and 'middle' farmers to the detriment not only of the old *hacendados* but also of the *ejidatarios*. Such policy is, of course, in line with the development of an industrial capitalist economy – in Mexico, as elsewhere.

Morelos, as always, spotlights the trend.

Like the rest of Mexico, it began to change. Factories sprang up, and highways were constructed. Moreover, it became a centre for cash crops – peanuts, rice and, of course, sugar cane. Zapata would not have been pleased. Over the years, the population of the state increased considerably. By 1960, the population was more than twice that of 1920; and by 1970, over fifty per cent of the inhabitants had come from elsewhere, or were the children of those from elsewhere.

In 1966, there were 32,000 *ejidatarios* in just over two hundred *ejidos*, comprising almost 300,000 hectares of fields, pasture and timber forests. But there were also 10,000 private proprietors and *rancheros*, often with tiny plots of uneconomical land. Between 1927 and 1967, the number of *ejidos* and *ejidatarios* doubled; and the number of hectares of land that they worked also more than doubled, but the pressure of population and, perhaps even more important, the lure of 'high' wages in the factories during the post-war boom, ineluctably drove the *peones* from the land.[29]

FEUDALISM in Mexico has gone. A new bourgeois, middle-class, has emerged, as well as its opposite, a propertyless, wage-earning proletariat. But there are still large numbers of *peones*, often living in appalling poverty. Indeed, in absolute numbers, due to the increase in population, there are more landless peasants in Mexico today than there were in 1910.

In October, 1972, Hugh O'Shaughnessy reported that 'the poor are getting relatively poorer, and the rich, richer in what is for the moment a businessman's paradise.'[30] He quoted Robert McNamara, president of the World Bank, as saying that in Mexico during the last twenty years, the richest ten per cent of the population had increased its share of the national wealth to just over half, while the poorest forty per cent had seen their slice of the national cake shrink to eleven per cent. And Luis Echeverria, in his inaugural presidential address, admitted that, after one hundred-and-fifty years of independence, very many Mexicans lived in 'lacerating poverty,' with not enough food, clothes or even drinking water. 'Let us produce more food, and get it to the poor man's table,' he added.[31] According to Dr. Bartolome Perez Ortiz, a nutrition expert at the Mexico City children's hospital, over seventy per cent of Mexican children suffered from malnutrition in 1974. Possibly, the situation has worsened since then.

For many years, however, neither the peasants nor the industrial workers attempted to do much about the situation. They had become apathetic, demoralised, even frightened. Mexican governments had become increasingly repressive. But by 1968 — the year of student and worker unrest throughout much of the world — Mexico began to stir.

'In 1968,' writes Victor Alba, 'more than halfway through Diaz Ordaz's term, which had been characterised by the widening of the economic gap between rich and poor, there was an outbreak of fury, and during it the president was attacked, cursed and booed. The Mexicans could hardly believe what occurred themselves.'[32]

In October, on the eve of the Olympic Games which were being held in Mexico City there was a student demonstration in the Plaza de Tlatelolco. Units of the army were called in to disperse it; over two hundred people were killed by the army (government sources claim that some of the troops were fired upon), and many hundreds were jailed, some for more than three years without trial. Accusations were also made to the effect that the trouble was stirred up by Russian-trained KGB agents. True or not, subsequent unrest in Mexico — particularly in the countryside — has been rooted in socio-economic conditions.

AFTER May 1969, numerous *Zapatista*-type groups were formed, and have been active in different parts of the country.

Early in 1973, for instance, a group of *guerrilleros* ambushed government troops in the Acapulco area on a number of occasions, killing a score or so. During the same year, there was considerable unrest in both the state of Puebla and in Puebla City itself. Following a series of land occupations and expropriations, the whole state was in turmoil.

There were numerous assassinations. Among those murdered, were three university professors who had supported the peasants. A number of *peones*, who had been occupying privately-owned land-holdings, were also murdered by fanatical rightist vigilante groups, encouraged, according to the *peones* by the local archbishop of the Catholic Church.

In the state of Guerrero, a guerrilla 'party of the poor' — which was not, in fact, a political party, but a *Zapatista*-type organisation — had considerable grassroots support among the peasants. The 'party of the poor' operated in the vast, and almost impenetrable, mountain areas between Acapulco on the Pacific Coast and eastern Morelos. Its armed 'wing' was called the 'brigade of peasant executioners.' The 'party of the poor' helped local *peones* to establish *ejido*-type co-operative farms. Its leader, the highly talented former school teacher, Lucio Cabanas, was finally shot by the army in December, 1974.

During 1975, large numbers of poor peasants developed a broad movement of 'illegal' occupations of lands throughout Guerrero, Hidalgo, Michoacan, Sonora and Tlaxcala. They were, in many instances, attacked by regular army units. Scores of them were killed and injured. In Michoacan, in January, 1976, forty-five families were driven from the lands which they had occupied. And during the first five months of the year, fifty *campesinos* were killed and over five hundred injured in clashes with government forces in various parts of the country. In November, two hundred landless peasants occupied four large *ranchos* in Culiacan.

In a desperate attempt to head off further unrest, the outgoing president, Luis Echeverria, expropriated about 100,000 hectares of private land in the state of Sonora for distribution to the peasants. The peasants had been seizing much of the land anyway! And they refused to give it back.

Nevertheless, by the end of 1977, land seizures began to slacken off.[33] Attempts have been made to build and organise autonomous labour unions. 'The change of tactics corresponds to a growing realisation by agricultural workers that local seizures or grants of tiny, individual plots of land, will never give them the power base they need to become self-sufficient . . .'[34] The *Coordinadora Campesino Revolucionaria Independent*, founded in Mexico City, co-ordinates groups from Colina, Morelos, Oaxaca, Pueblo, Sinaloa, Veracruz and elsewhere. A number of traditional agricultural unions, as well as two or three so-called 'revolutionary' parties, also vide for the *campesinos'* support.

In one form or another, the struggle continues . . . .

And in the words of Mary Charlesworth: 'The Mexican revolution is still incomplete, as great inequalities in wealth exist and the peasant-land problem is still unsolved. But at least there is the ideal of the revolution to struggle towards, and this is important for the Mexican temperament.'[35] The spirit of *Zapatismo* lives on.

1. William Howells, *Man in the Beginning,* pp274-275.
2. Robert Claiborne, *The First Americans,* p15.
3. Jonathan N. Leonard, *The First Farmers,* p50.
4. Ibid, p139.
5. George C. Vaillant, *The Aztecs of Mexico*, pp65-66.
6. Henry Bamford Parkes, *A History of Mexico*, pp3-4.
7. Ibid, p7.
8. Lewis Henry Morgan, *Ancient Society*, p192.
9. Vaillant, p127.
10. Ibid, p128.
11. William H. Prescott, *History of the Conquest of Mexico*, p19, (footnote).
12. Peter Kropotkin, *Mutual Aid*, p110.
13. Ricardo Flores Magon, *Land and Liberty*, p22.
14. John Gunther, *Inside Latin America*, p67.
15. Victor Alba, *A Concise History of Mexico,* p38.
16. Parkes, p82.
17. Eric R. Wolf, *Peasant Wars of the Twentieth Century*, p4.
18. Ibid, p16.
19. Gerrit Huizer, *Peasant Rebellion in Latin America*, p34.
20. Alba, p158. Ramon Beteta, *Programma Economico y Social de Mexico*, p26.
21. Rafael Segovia, *Latin America and the Caribbean — A Handbook*, p155, and *Encyclopaedia Britannica,* Vol. 15, p.336.
22. William W. Johnson, *Heroic Mexico*, p386.
23. Parkes, p343.
24. Gunther, pp69-70, and Segovia, p157.
25. Parkes, p343.
26. Beteta and others in *Programma.*
27. Josue de Castro, *Geography of Hunger*, pp95-96.
28. Segovia, p161.
29. John Womack, Jr., *Zapata and the Mexican Revolution*, pp383-385.

30. *The Observer,* (London), 1.10.72.
31. *The Guardian,* (London), 4.4.73.
32. Alba, p209.
33. *Open Road* (Vancouver), The Fall, 1977.
34. Ibid, and *Interrogations* (Torino), No. 10, 1977.
35. Mary Charlesworth, *Revolution In Perspective,* p49.

REFERENCES AND SOURCES

ALBA, Victor, *A Concise History of Mexico,* London 1973.
ATKIN, Ronald, *Revolution! Mexico 1910-20,* London, 1969.
BARBA GONZALEZ, Silvano, *Emiliano Zapata,* Mexico City, 1960.
BETETA, Ramon, *Programma Economico y Social de Mexico,* Mexico City, 1935.
BLAISDELL, Lowell L, *The Desert Revolution,* Madison, 1962.
CERVANTES, Federico, *Francisco Villa y la Revolucion,* Mexico City, 1960.
COLLOBI, Lucia R. and RAGGHIANTI, Carlo L., *National Museum of Anthropology – Mexico City,* Milan, 1970.
CLAIBORN, Robert, *The First Americans,* Amsterdam, 1976.
CHARLESWORTH, Mary, *Revolution in Perspective,* Weerts, 1972.
CUMBERLAND, Charles C., *Mexican Revolution: Genesis Under Madero,* Austin, Texas, 1952.
CUMBERLAND, Charles C., *Mexican Revolution: The Constitutional Years,* Austin, Texas, 1972.
DEAS, Malcolm and CARR, Ramond, *Mexico: The Ragged Revolution, (History of the 20th Century, No. 9),* London, n/d.
DE CASTRO, Josue, *Geography of Hunger,* London, 1952.
DIAZ SOTO Y GAMA, Antonio, *La Revolucion Agraria Del Sur y Emiliano Zapata,* Mexico City, 1960.
DUNN, Harry H., *The Crimson Jester: Zapata of Mexico,* London, 1934.
ENCYCLOPAEDIA BRITANNICA, Volume 15, *Mexico,* Chicago, 1973 edition.
ENCYCLOPAEDIA BRITANNICA, Volume 25, *Emiliano Zapata,* Chicago, 1973 edition.
GUNTHER, John, *Inside Latin America,* New York, 1941.
HOBSBAWM, Eric J., *Bandits,* London 1972.
HOWELLS, William, *Man in the Beginning,* London, 1956.
HUIZER, Gerrit, *Peasant Rebellion in Latin America,* London, 1973.

JOHNSON, William W., *Heroic Mexico: The Narrative History of a Twentieth Century Revolution*, New York, 1968.

KING, Rosa E., *Tempest Over Mexico*, London, 1936.

KROPOTKIN, *Mutual Aid*, London, 1939.

LINCOLN, John, *One Man's Mexico*, London, 1967.

MAGANA, Gildardo, *Emiliano Zapata y El Agrarismo en Mexico*, 5v, Mexico, 1951-52.

MAGON, Ricardo Flores, *Semilla Libertaria (Articulos)*, Mexico F.D. 1923.

MAGON, Ricardo Flores, *Land and Liberty*, (compiled and edited by David Poole), Sanday, Orkney, 1977.

LEONARD, Jonathan N., *The First Farmers*, Amsterdam, 1974.

MILLON, Robert P., *Zapata: The Ideology of a Peasant Revolutionary*, New York, 1969.

MOATS, Leone B., *Thunder in Their Veins*, London, 1933.

MONTEMAR, Rene G.D. and ALFONSO, Roberto, *Emiliano Zapata*, Alburquerque, 1973.

MORGAN, Lewis H., *Ancient Society*, Calcutta, n/d.

PARKES, Henry Bamford, *A History of Mexico*, London, 1962.

PINCHON, Edgcum, *Viva Villa!*, London, 1933.

PINCHON, Edgcum, *Zapata The Unconquerable*, New York, 1941.

PRESCOTT, William H., *History of the Conquest of Mexico*, London, 1843.

REED, John, *Insurgent Mexico*, Berlin, 1974.

SANTILLAN, Diego Abad de, *Ricardo Flores Magon*, Mexico F.D., 1925.

SEGOVIA, Rafael, *Latin America and the Caribbean — A Handbook*, London, 1968.

STEVENSON, Jack, *Zapata and the Mexican Revolution*,(pamphlet), London, 1970.

TANNENBAUM, Frank, *The Mexican Agrarian Revolution*, Washington, D.C., 1930.

TURNER, Kenneth John, *Barbarous Mexico*, Chicago, 1910.

VAILLANT, George C., *The Aztecs of Mexico*, London, 1950.

WOLF, Eric R., *Peasant Wars of the Twentieth Century*, London, 1971.

WOLFE, Betram D., and RIVERA, Diego, *Portrait of Mexico*, New York, 1937.

WOODCOCK, George, *Anarchism: A History of Libertarian Ideas and Movements*, London, 1962.

WOMACK JR., John, *Zapata and the Mexican Revolution*, New York, 1969.

ZAVALA, Silvio, *The Contact of Cultures in Mexican History: Interrelations of Culture*, (UNESCO), Paris, 1953.

THE OTHER MEXICO

The North American Triangle Completed

John W. Warnock

This book examines these changes and shows how the Mexican people have fought against them in their efforts to create an alternative, more humane society.

Finding out what is really happening in a country requires in-depth research and that is just what Warnock has provided. The book ends with a superb collection of photos.
Briarpatch

321 pages, photographs by Elaine Brière
Paperback 1-55164-028-7 $23.99
Hardcover 1-55164-029-5 $52.99

FREE TRADE

Neither Free Nor About Trade

Christopher D. Merrett

Merrett forces the rhetoric surrounding free trade into a confrontation with the facts: rising unemployment, falling wages, and the dismantling of Canada's social programs.
Barney Warf
A well-documented, convincingly argued warning to Canadians about the supposed "benefits" of free trade.
Richard Peet

320 pages, index
Paperback 1-55164-044-9 $23.99
Hardcover 1-55164-045-7 $52.99

MASK OF DEMOCRACY*

Labour Suppression in Mexico Today

Dan LaBotz

Following scores of interviews with Mexican workers, labour union officials, women's organizations, lawyers, and human rights activists, Dan LaBotz presents this study of the suppression of workers' rights in Mexico.

Now we can see why the situation for Mexican workers continues to get worse.
Mexican Acton Network on Free Trade

223 pages, index. An ILRERF Book
Paperback ISBN: 1-895431-58-1 $19.99
Hardcover ISBN: 1-895431-59-X $48.99

BLACK ROSE BOOKS

has also published the following books of related interest

Mask of Democracy, Labour Suppression in Mexico Today, *by Dan LaBotz*
The Other Mexico: The North American Triangle Completed,
    by John W. Warnock
Mexico: Land and Liberty, Anarchist Influences in the Mexican
    Revolution, *by Ricardo Flores Magon*
Green Guerrillas: Environmental Conflicts and Iniatives in Latin
    America and the Carribbean, *edited by Helen Collinson*
Wollaston: People Resisting Genocide, *by Miles Goldstick*
The New Resource Wars: Native Struggles Against Multinational
    Corporations, *by Al Gedicks*
Free Trade: Neither Free Nor About Trade, *by Christopher Merrett*
Turning the Tide: The US and Latin America, *by Noam Chomsky*
Complicity: Human Rights and Canadian Foreign Policy: The Case of East
    Timor, *by Sharon Scharfe*
Anarchist Organization: The History of the F.A.I., *by Juan Gomez Casas*
The Cuban Revolution: A Critical Perspective, *by Sam Dolgoff*
Local Places: In the Age of the Global City, *edited by Roger Keil, Gerda Wekerle,
    and David Bell*
Durruti: The People Armed, *by Abel Paz*
Women and Counter-Power, *edited by Yolande Cohen*
Myth of the Market: Promises and Illusions, *by Jeremy Seabrook*
The Political Economy of International Labour Migration, *by Hassan Gardezi*

send for a free catalogue of all our titles
BLACK ROSE BOOKS
C.P. 1258
Succ. Place du Parc
Montréal, Québec
H3W 2R3 Canada

To order books in North America: (phone) 1-800-565-9523
(fax) 1-800-221-9985
In Europe: (phone) 44-081-986-4854 (fax) 44-081-533-5821

Web site address: http://www.web.net/blackrosebooks

Printed by the workers of   —
Veilleux Impression À Demande Inc.
Boucherville, Quebec
for Black Rose Books Ltd.